RITUAL AND MAGIC

MARVELS & MYSTERIES

RITUAL AND MAGIC

PARRAGON

Published in 1997 by Parragon
Unit 13-17 Avonbridge Trading Estate,
Atlantic Road, Avonmouth, Bristol BS11 9QD
All rights reserved

ISBN 0-75252-188-8

Printed and bound in Italy

CONTENTS

INTRODUCTION

Alongside the conventional history we learn in school, the tales of ballots and battles, popes and prelates, industry and issues, there has been another tale unfolding. This is the history of inner space, of the way people have developed their minds and their psychic potential, attempting to get a deeper understanding of the realities underlying the world they live in and to exercise greater power over it and themselves; it is the history of ritual and magic. This book presents scenes and personalities from this alternative history, dating from Ancient Egypt to the present day. It looks at the roots of occult traditions such as sex magic, witchcraft and cabalism, and the way they have been applied over the centuries for good and ill, and tells the stories of famous magicians such as Paracelsus, Eliphas Levi and Aleister Crowley.

Magic can be defined simply as the attempt to manipulate physical reality and consciousness by an effort of will. The 'real' world is seen as essentially a creation of our minds, an illusion in Buddhist terms, and the magician attempts to change the world by literally changing his and other people's minds. Ritual is the great tool of magic; indeed, there is a case for saying that all rituals have a magical core, even those at the centre of those great religions that damn all magic as a manifestation of evil. The key elements of all ritual and ceremony – rhythm and repetition, special clothing, prescribed actions and words, incantations, incense and symbolism – are all capable of affecting the state of mind of those taking part, and so affect reality.

in thought, word and deed – is an essential prerequisite for spiritual advancement. Typical of this viewpoint was the medieval compiler of *The Sworn Book of Honorius*, a textbook of ritual magic, who solemnly advised his readers to 'be penitent and truly confessed of all sins, forbearing all female enticements . . . for it is better to live with a bear or a lion in its den than live with a woman'.

Other occultists and mystics have adopted a diametrically opposite point of view, regarding sexual activity as an authentic sacrament – 'the outward and visible sign of an inward and spiritual grace'. Such a sacramental use of sexual intercourse can supposedly be employed as a means of acquiring occult power and, at its highest, may lead to the ultimate goal of the mystic union with the divine, so it is said.

Among those mystics who have believed this are the 16th-century writers Cornelius Agrippa and Aratus. The former described copulation as 'full of magical endowment', while Aratus claimed that:

'As the physical union of man and woman leads to the fruit from the composition of each, in the same way the interior and secret association of man and woman is the copulation of the male and female soul, and is appointed for the production of fitting fruit of the divine life.'

ALCHEMICAL CONNECTIONS

Sexual symbolism was in common use among alchemists and some of them interpreted such symbolic phrases as 'the marriage of the Red King and the White Queen' not only chemically but also sexually. Some went so far as to attempt to manufacture the Philosopher's Stone – the mysterious substance that would transmute base metal into gold – from human semen. Thus 18th-century German records, quoted by Christopher McIntosh in his historical study of Rosicrucian societies, tell of an alchemical group that engaged in experiments of this sort. The leader of the group, an officer of high rank in the Austrian army, collected the raw material for this curious research by paying soldiers to masturbate.

The experiment ended in disaster. The soldiers under the officer's command were so enthusiastic to supplement their meagre pay that they neglected their military duties in order to engage in almost incessant masturbation. Eventually, the regimental surgeon became aware of what was going on. The alchemical officer was reported to his commanding general and dismissed from the service. And to add insult to injury, the alchemists failed in all their attempts at transmutation.

Neither a ludicrous episode such as this nor the occasional confidence trickster who uses mysticism and the occult as an excuse to engage in sexual fun and games should be taken as an indication that all who believe sex to be capable of leading to authentic religious experience are mad or perverted.

In the West, there has always been a complex inter-relationship between religion and magic on the one hand and human sexuality on the other. Almost all mystical symbol-systems, from astrology to the Tarot, have been given sexual interpretations. Even *The Bible* has been subjected to the same treatment by some commentators. Eliphas Lévi, for

SEX, SIN AND SACRAMENT

THE SEX DRIVE HAS BEEN EXALTED BY SOME OCCULTISTS, EVEN BECOMING THE INSTRUMENT AND OBJECT OF CERTAIN MAGICAL PRACTICES

There has always been a curious ambivalence in occult attitudes towards physical sexuality. Thus some occultists and psychics have looked upon any and every sexual feeling or activity as pertaining to mankind's 'lower nature'. According to this school of thought, absolute chastity – purity

In the engraving above, a virgin is prepared for sacrifice during a black mass, with the goat-horned figure of the 'priest' representing the Devil in the background.

other magicians. Those who hold this theory point out that poltergeist activity is usually associated with a disturbed adolescent who is unable to 'earth' his or her sexual energies with a partner of the opposite sex. The occult writer Benjamin Walker has gone so far as to claim that:

'Psychic researchers have repeatedly established that the centre of poltergeist activity is often a persistent masturbator, and they believe it possible that the biomagnetic energy drawn by the poltergeist is obtained during the release of sexual tension, when the masturbator reaches his or her climax. Excessive masturbation... has also been cited as the reason for other unexplained psychic occurrences...'

❚❚ SOME OF THOSE OCCULTISTS AND PSYCHICAL RESEARCHERS WHO ASSERT THAT THE SUBTLE FORCES OF THE SEANCE ROOM AND THE SEXUAL CURRENTS OF THE LIBIDO ARE MANIFESTATIONS OF ONE MYSTERIOUS ENERGY ALSO BELIEVE THAT IT CAN BE TRANSFERRED FROM ONE PERSON TO ANOTHER. ❚❚

instance, believed that the fall of Man, as described in *Genesis,* was sexual in nature: indeed, the 'original sin', which laid a perpetual curse on humanity, was seen as being Adam and Eve's first coupling. Madame Blavatsky, founder of the Theosophical Society, went even further: according to her, the first five books of *The Bible* are 'the symbolical narrative of the sexes, and an apotheosis of phallicism'. By 'phallicism', she meant the worship of the male sexual organ as a manifestation of the divine.

The potency of sex is the theme of Satana, above, engraved in 1896 by the artist Fidus who worked in Berlin. The woman is alluring, yet also strangely menacing, and the man seems to be in torment. His pose is somehow reminiscent of the crucifixion, and the title of the work makes an explicit link with magical sexual ritual.

UNMENTIONABLES

Unlikely as Madame Blavatsky's assertion may seem, there could be a modicum of truth in it. Some students of the *Talmud*, the lengthy compilation of ancient Jewish commentaries, would agree. According to them, the 'Ark of the Covenant', the holy chest made of acacia wood that the Israelites carried during their long wanderings and eventually placed in the Temple in Jerusalem, contained a sacred stone carved in the shape of the conjoined male and female sexual organs. There would be nothing particularly surprising in this, for similar objects have been venerated by many cults. The ancient Greek 'mysteries', or initiation rituals, carried out at Eleusis, for instance, involved a rite called 'carrying things not to be mentioned'. The unmentionable things in question seem to have been a stone model of an erect penis and a hollow stone, symbolising the womb of the goddess Demeter, who ruled over agriculture and fertility.

Some occultists believe that a mysterious psychic energy produces all the phenomena of the seance room, from table turning to spirit materialisation, and is, at root, identical with the energies that find their outlet in sex. It is the 'orgone' of Wilhelm Reich, the 'Od' of the 19th-century mesmerists, and the 'astral light' of Paracelsus and

The marriage of the Red King and the White Queen, right, from Splendor solis, a 16th-century manuscript by Salomon Trismosin, represents conventionally the combination of sulphur (male) and mercury (female). The Philosopher's Stone, which was believed to transmute base metals into gold, was said to be born of this union. Some alchemists interpreted such symbolism quite literally, and regarded sexual activity as necessary to the making of the elusive Stone.

Whether or not excessive masturbation can be productive of psychic happenings, there seems little doubt that at least some outbreaks of poltergeist activity are triggered by sexual mishaps or unhappy and complex emotional involvements. Take, for example, the so-called 'great Amherst mystery' – the poltergeist haunting that astonished the inhabitants of Nova Scotia, Canada, in the autumn of 1878. It centred on 18-year-old Esther Cox. 'Esther Cox you are mine to kill', said writing that mysteriously appeared on the wall of the girl's bedroom. The haunting featured just about every type of poltergeist activity, from outbreaks of fire and stone-throwing to Esther's stomach swelling to enormous size. This last effect was presumably the result of swallowing air, or some internal fermentation, for she reverted to her normal shapeliness after 'a loud report, like a clap of thunder but without any characteristic rumble'. This must have been one of the noisiest poltergeist bangs ever, for Esther's mother leapt to the conclusion that her home had been struck by a meteorite and rushed to the bedroom of her youngest children to see if all was well with them. She found them sleeping peacefully and the house undamaged.

If, as seems likely, the poltergeist's 'thunderclap' was Esther breaking wind with immense vigour, one is forced to consider the possibility that the knocks, bangs and drummings associated with poltergeists sometimes have a similar origin. It is perhaps significant that the noises made by the 17th-century poltergeist known as the drummer of Tedworth were on at least one occasion accompanied by a 'mysterious sulphurous smell', which 'those present found very offensive'. No such smells were reported by those who witnessed the Amherst hauntings: perhaps there were none or, more likely, Victorian sensibilities prevented them from being mentioned.

These allegedly paranormal happenings were almost certainly triggered by an experience undergone by Esther on 28 August 1878, exactly eight days before the supposed poltergeist first manifested itself. It involved Esther's boyfriend, a certain Bob McNeal.

It is probable that for some time Bob had been making overt sexual advances to Esther; for on the night of 27 August, she had a nightmare, replete with Freudian symbolism, clearly expressing the girl's fear of male sexuality. In this dream, all Esther's relatives had been magically transformed into huge bears with red eyes. When she opened the front door of her home, she was horrified to see hundreds of black bulls, blood dripping from their muzzles, converging on the house. She slammed the door shut and bolted it, but the bulls continued their advance, butting their huge horns against the house. The building shook under the concerted assault, and then Esther awoke.

On the evening of the day following this ominous dream, Bob McNeal took Esther for a drive in a two-seater buggy, which he had borrowed or hired. They drove together into the surrounding wooded countryside. Bob reined in the horse and began to make amorous advances to Esther, urging her to walk into the woods with him. When she consistently refused – it would seem that she was prepared to indulge in a little light petting in the

buggy but nothing more – McNeal lost his temper. He pulled out a pistol, pointed it at the girl's head, and ordered her to accompany him into the woods. She still refused, and for a moment it seemed that McNeal would shoot her dead. Fortunately, however, another vehicle approached, the alarmed McNeal pocketed his pistol, snatched up the horse's reins, and drove Esther to her home. That night, he left Amherst, presumably in fear of being charged with attempted rape, and was never heard of again.

In a sense, however, he remained with Esther for many years. The sexual cravings and fears that McNeal had aroused seem to have built up in Esther a pressure of psychic energy – a sort of

Hereward Carrington, psychical researcher, **right,** *traced and interviewed Esther Cox, a famous poltergeist victim who, many years before, had been plagued by disturbances at her home,* **below right,** *in Amherst, Nova Scotia. The house was almost wrecked by some of the outbreaks. Carrington found that the phenomena had not in fact recurred since Esther's marriage – possibly due to release of her sexual energies.*

impending libidinal thunderstorm. Failing to find an outlet in the ecstasy of orgasm, it is thought to have powered the spontaneous combustions, levitations and other psychic wonders that astonished the citizens of Amherst.

Many years later, Hereward Carrington, the psychical investigator, traced and interviewed Esther, by then married and living in the United States. She was reluctant to talk about the past, but made a most significant admission. From the day of her wedding, she said, 'the power' had left her; she was again a stranger to the paranormal.

Some of those occultists and psychical researchers who assert that the 'subtle forces' of the seance room and the sexual currents of the libido are manifestations of one mysterious energy also believe that it can be transferred from one person to another. In this way, so it is suggested, the old can, accidentally or by design, draw in the life force from a younger person for their own benefit.

The use of this curious psychic technique has a long history. It is often called 'Shunamitism', a term that is derived from an incident recorded in the *Old Testament:*

'Now King David was old and stricken in years... he gat no heat. Wherefore his servants said unto him, "Let there be sought for my lord the king a young virgin... and let her lie in thy bosom, that my lord the king may get heat". So they sought for a fair damsel throughout all the coasts of Israel, and found Abishag, a Shunammite, and brought her to the king. And the damsel was very fair and cherished the king, and ministered to him... '

Abishag regularly slept with David, so it is said, but did not have sexual intercourse with him, for this would have 'earthed' the life force and frustrated their intention.

// LATIN HISTORIANS RECORD THE REMARKABLE CASE OF L.CLAUDIUS HERMIPPUS. WHEN HE REACHED THE AGE OF 70, HE BEGAN TO FEEL A WANING OF HIS PHYSICAL AND MENTAL POWERS. HE IMMEDIATELY BEGAN TO SLEEP WITH YOUNG VIRGINS – THOUGH WITHOUT SEXUAL ACTIVITY. HIS TOMBSTONE RECORDED THAT HE LIVED TO BE 115, OWING TO THE EMANATIONS OF YOUNG MAIDENS. **//**

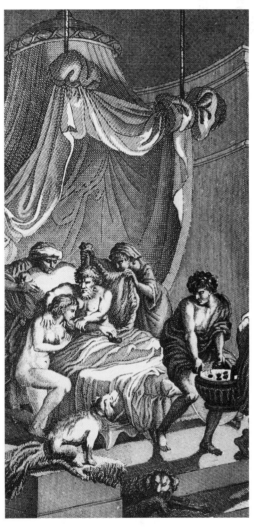

Barbarossa (Frederick I of Germany), above, revived his failing energies by bodily contact with young boys. The cure may have been surprisingly successful: legend even has it that he did not die but merely sleeps. King David's tonic, right, meanwhile, is said to have been the embrace of Abishag.

The same technique was used in classical Greece and Rome, seemingly with considerable success. Latin historians record, for example, the remarkable case of a certain L. Claudius Hermippus. When he reached the age of 70, he began to feel a waning of his physical and mental powers. He immediately began to sleep with young virgins – though, like King David, without sexual activity. His tombstone recorded that he lived to the age of 115, owing to 'the emanations of young maidens, causing great wonder to all physicians'.

Many European rulers of the Middle Ages practised Shunamitism, sometimes in a homosexual variant. Thus, the Emperor Barbarossa held young boys against his stomach and genitals in order to 'savour and absorb their energy'; and Pope Innocent VIII, the immediate predecessor of the Borgia pope, Alexander VI, employed healthy young children to stroke him and thus transfer their more youthful energy to him.

Some physicians of the time held that this life energy was strongly concentrated in youthful blood; and Ficino, a Platonic philosopher who also practised medicine, even suggested that vampirism should be employed by those enfeebled by age. The old, he said, should drink fresh blood drawn from youthful veins 'after the manner of leeches'.

Shunamitism survived into the 18th century and, in both Paris and London, was practised on a commercial basis. For example, a certain Madame Janus of Paris owned a successful establishment that at one time was reputed to give employment to over 40 virgins. A client's course of treatment lasted for three weeks. Each night, he was given a 'magical bath' containing herbs, then massaged with aromatic oils, and finally tucked into bed between two virgins, one blonde and one brunette. The treatment was, of course, expensive and had to be paid for in advance. In addition, Madame Janus insisted that each client deposit a substantial sum of money with her. This was to be forfeited by any

man who was so rejuvenated that he deflowered one of his sleeping partners.

A similar establishment, the 'temple of Aurora', was conducted in London by Mrs Anna Fawkland, whose clients were reputed to include elderly aristocrats, such as Lords Buckingham and Cornwallis.

A belief in the efficacy of this almost vampire-like technique for acquiring psychosexual energy was also among the strangely assorted articles of faith of Heinrich Himmler, sinister chief of the Nazi SS. Himmler, as well as carrying out his unpleasant duties with dry efficiency, spent much time thinking about such unlikely problems as the mystic symbolism of Gothic architecture and 'the occult significance of the Etonian top hat'. In 1940, he became concerned about the number of Luftwaffe pilots who died from exposure after parachuting into the North Sea. He decided that, if such pilots were picked up while still alive, they would probably recover if they were placed between the bodies of naked girls. To test this hypothesis, SS physicians carried out a series of cruel experiments in which concentration camp inmates were placed in tanks of freezing water until they became unconscious and were then put to bed between naked girls.

The efforts of the women revived several victims to a point at which they achieved coitus. But this depraved parody of Shunamitism did not lead to a higher recovery rate overall than did orthodox methods of warming the experimental subjects.

RITUAL MAGIC

just like their neighbours. But there is no denying that their private beliefs are sometimes odd to the point of what some would describe as eccentricity. They see the Universe as a living being, its visible appearance veiling its real nature; and they regard symbol and allegory, dream and vision as more truly conveying ultimate reality than all the equations of the mathematician and the astrophysicist.

The various physical and psychological techniques employed today by magicians are quite as strange as the beliefs that inspire them. The modern magician, for instance, will hold his body in painful and unlikely postures for long periods of time. He will spend weeks in the visualisation of, and meditation upon, some simple coloured symbol – perhaps a red triangle or a yellow square. He will half-choke himself with the smoke of exotic incenses; he will whirl like a spinning top until he falls senseless to the ground; he may clad himself in strange robes and stand, amid circles and symbols, chanting the words of evocation that, so he believes, will bring the gods down to earth and help him, in turn, become supremely powerful.

It has been suggested, however, that many others besides an occult minority have practised ritual magic this century. Politicians and clergymen,

The art of creating changes in consciousness in accordance with will is today practised in every great city of the Western world. For a body of theory and practice that the confident mid-Victorian materialist regarded as a sad relic of the irrational past, doomed to be swept into the dustbin of history, has in fact survived and flourished. It is impossible to be sure just how many men and women regularly engage in ritual magic, but there is a fair number certainly, for several thriving businesses exist to supply their needs. In England, for example, there are mail order firms issuing catalogues that contain a large selection of magical paraphernalia: swords, daggers, ceremonial candles and incenses appropriate to every type of magical rite are included.

Many modern magicians appear to live ordinary enough lives. They have jobs and families, they mow their lawns, go on holiday, and pay their taxes

Few political or military movements in modern times have used special effects, such as lights, music and stirring speech, in order to manipulate the minds of the masses as successfully as the Nazis, top left. No detail was overlooked; and the blood banner that had been carried by Hitler in the putsch of 1923 was used in every ceremony consecrating new swastika banners, as shown above. Yet total concentration on blood and death was to backfire – their vision of martial glory ending in the snows of Stalingrad, above left, and the ruins of Berlin.

speakers at protest meetings and strike leaders – all, so it is argued, *unconsciously* employ magical techniques. They have learned from others, or have themselves developed on the basis of experience, the same methods of altering consciousness employed by modern magicians: but while the magician is usually concerned only with altering the state of consciousness of himself and perhaps a few close associates, the politician or priest is intent on altering the feelings and actions of hundreds, thousands, or, in the case of such revolutionaries as Adolf Hitler and Eva Peron, maybe many millions of people.

MAGICAL PERFORMANCES

Ritual magicians employ light, colour, sound and highly theatrical spectacle to achieve what some have called 'one-pointedness' – in other words, the directing of the mind towards one particular idea, or universal factor. If, for example, a contemporary magician wants to concentrate his consciousness upon, and flood his mind and spirit with, the ideal of benevolent power, he will 'invoke Jupiter' – that is, he will either play the chief part or be the only actor in a 'mystery play' in which he identifies himself with this god and surrounds himself with theatrical 'props' that are traditionally associated with the deity and his attributes.

Inside his magic circle, he will outline a square or a four-pointed star – four is the number sacred to Jupiter – with chalks or paints of Jupiter's colours – violet, purple and shades of blue. He will decorate his 'temple', the room in which he carries out his ceremonial workings, with sprays of oak and poplar leaves, associated with the god since classical times. In his censer, or incense burner, cedar wood and saffron, recognised as perfumes of Jupiter, will smoulder on a bed of glowing charcoal. And if he is one of that small minority of ritualists who employ mind-altering drugs, some opium may also have been placed in the censer or he will have smoked opium before the ceremony.

Once this setting for the Jupiterian mystery play has been prepared, the magician will begin to act out his role, identifying himself with the god in exactly the same way that a 'method' actor identifies himself with the character he is portraying. Every word the magician will say during his performance, every act he will carry out, every 'Name of Power' he chants, will be associated with the Jupiterian principle of benevolent power. And by the end of the rite, the magician's mind will – if he has been successful – be filled with that principle to the exclusion of all else.

// NOBODY IN CREATION IS CLEVERER

THAN THE HUMAN BEING. POSSESSED

OF THE MOST ACCESSIBLE

TECHNIQUES, HE CAN MAKE ALL

CREATION HIS SERVANT... //

KO HUNG, REJOINDER

TO POPULAR CONCEPTIONS

Today, too, the ritual magician, above, invokes the gods by flooding his mind with the concept of supreme power and surrounding himself with traditional symbols.

Exactly the same system – that of using ceremony to alter emotions and consciousness – is also employed in many respects by politicians and statesmen. Take, for example, the May Day processions that would take place in any Communist country. The fluttering red flags, the pictures of revolutionary heroes and martyrs borne aloft, the thousands of clenched fists and stamping feet, and the dais upon which stand the party leaders beneath vast romanticised portraits of Marx, Engels and Lenin – all are the political equivalents of the furnishings and decorations of the magician's temple, and there is no doubt that the consciousness of the onlookers and participants in the revolutionary ceremony becomes changed. Drab working lives, inadequate housing and food, fears for the future are all forgotten. Instead, the people feel themselves to be part of a great marching army, a rushing tide of progress destined, by the laws of history, to smash down all that stands in its way, in the attempt to create a new and better world.

Perhaps the greatest masters of such 'political ritual magic' were the leaders of the Nazi Party. Indeed, some occultists have gone so far as to suggest that Adolf Hitler and his closest associates had studied the techniques of occult ceremony, deliberately applying them to political purposes. This theory has long been debated, with no firm conclusions forthcoming. At one period of his early

life, the future Führer undoubtedly read a great deal of occult literature; and what does seem certain is that the Nazi's Nuremberg Rallies were extremely formalised, elaborately staged ceremonies, designed to exert a particular effect upon the minds both of the participants and of those who later saw films of them.

Fanfares from assembled trumpeters in traditional costume or the theatrical black and silver uniforms of the SS, the stirring marches played to the gathering crowds, and the concerts of Wagner's music that usually preceded each rally – all caused mental associations with the ideas of Germanic myth and tradition, military glory and National Socialism (Nazism). At each rally, the massed swastika banners – black, white and red, traditionally a colour combination associated with war, terror and death – brought into the consciousness of the participants the entire Nazi ideology. The high point and prime ritual of the rallies, meanwhile – Hitler ceremonially consecrating new swastika banners by clasping them to the 'blood banner' that had been carried by him and others in the unsuccessful Munich *putsch* of 1923 – was the most potent element in the Nazis' loathsome 'mystery play'. Indeed, the emotions conveyed by it were such that the minds of living Nazis were, in a sense, linked with the thoughts and actions of National Socialist martyrs. One might say it was almost a sacrament.

The magical and quasi-religious aspects of these rallies were emphasised by the fact that their climax always came after darkness and took place in what Albert Speer, the Nazi technocrat, described as 'a cathedral of light' – an open space surrounded by upright beams, reminiscent of the pillars of Gothic architecture, emanating from anti-aircraft searchlights pointed directly up towards the sky.

The Nuremberg Rallies undoubtedly achieved their intended effects. The overwhelming majority of those who either witnessed or participated in them found their minds overflowing with ideas of glory, military struggle and self-sacrifice for the good of the Aryan race. Even if an occultist of great expertise had spent years in devising a ritual to invoke Mars, he would have been unlikely to have

Giant idealised portraits of the former USSR's officially approved heroes, above, served at May Day celebrations to direct the minds of the participants towards a single goal – furtherance of the Communist state.

come up with anything more effective than the ceremonies employed at Nuremberg.

Some occultists claim that those who raise the old gods from the depths of the unconscious run the risk of being destroyed by them. Certainly, many of the young men who invoked Mars at Nuremberg eventually fell as sacrifices – at Stalingrad, at Kursk, and in the fire and smoke of besieged Berlin.

At the present day, no statesman or politician conducts, consciously or otherwise, 'magical' ceremonies either as impressive or as sinister as those performed at Nuremberg. But similar use of light, colour and sound to alter the thought and feelings of an audience can be discerned in other aspects of contemporary life, in religious celebrations, and even in rock concerts. It has even been said that anyone who saw the late Janis Joplin in action in many ways witnessed a ritual evocation of the spirit of Venus quite as effective as any carried out by magicians, past or present.

" MAGIC IS IN EXISTENCE IN EVERY CULTURE IN THE WORLD – AND IS, IN ADDITION, STRIKINGLY UNIFIED DESPITE THE DIVERSITY OF CULTURES – BECAUSE IT IS A REFLECTION OF ETERNAL PRINCIPLES AND AS SUCH MUST EXIST SO LONG AS THERE ARE CULTURES. *"*

ARTHUR VERSLUIS,
THE PHILOSOPHY OF MAGIC

The late Janis Joplin, right, gave electric stage performances that embodied – unknowingly, it is thought – all the elements of an invocation of Venus.

The Papyrus of the goddess Anhai from one of the Egyptian Books of the Dead, left, shows Anhai's soul being weighed against truth and justice, represented as a feather. Horus, Anubis and Thoth are seen attending the weighing, in animal disguise.

The Magician from a Tarot pack, designed for Aleister Crowley by Frieda Harris, below, features Thoth in his guises as Hermes and as a baboon.

ECHOES OF ANCIENT EGYPT

A DISTANT CIVILISATION PERSISTS IN EXERTING A POTENT SPELL ON OUR IMAGINATION, INSPIRING MANY OCCULT SYSTEMS

When Aleister Crowley, the 'Beast of Revelation' and magus, published his commentary on the Tarot pack, he called it *The Book of Thoth* – proclaiming, as many other mystics and magicians have done, that it encapsulates the arcane wisdom of the ancient Egyptians.

Thoth was the scribe of the gods, who figured prominently in the ceremony of the 'weighing of the heart', the central ritual in the passage of a dead person's spirit from this world to the next. At this moment of trial, when Anubis, the jackal-headed god of the dead, laid the dead person's heart in one pan of a pair of scales to check that it balanced against a feather, representing justice and truth, Thoth stood by to record the result.

Thoth had another role, however, one more tantalising than the straightforward task of keeping the register of those who could enter into the realms of bliss. He was the god of knowledge and of wisdom. And by the easiest of extensions, he became the god of magic. The ancient Egyptians believed that Thoth had set down, in books 'written with his own hand', the most potent secrets of all. Indeed, Crowley and other modern necromancers have venerated Thoth as a continuing source of occult

Seth, below, the renegade brother of the god Osiris, was jealous of his superior power, killed and then dismembered him, scattering the remains all over the land. Their confrontation continues to fascinate occult scholars as the archetypal battle between forces of good and evil.

knowledge, thus enhancing the appeal of those rituals and magical systems that draw on Egyptian symbolism.

As long ago as 1781, a minor French scholar named Antoine Court de Gébelin claimed, with absolutely no foundation other than his imagination, that the 22 trumps of the Tarot pack preserved the secret teachings of the Egyptians, deliberately disguised to prevent exploitation by the uninitiated. The notion was happily accepted by later magicians, such as Eliphas Lévi in the 19th century. At around the same time, Count Cagliostro founded his Egyptian Rite of Masonry; for meetings, he used a temple room in Paris, furnished with statues of Isis and Anubis. Mozart, in his opera *The Magic Flute*, had also linked freemasonry with ancient Egypt and the mysteries of Isis and Osiris.

Ancient Egypt easily stimulates the occult imagination. For a start, there are the remains of an ancient and mystifying civilisation whose great works – the pyramids and temples ranged along the

Nile – suggest the use of powers and techniques that still amaze us in the technological late 20th century. There is, too, the accent on death, or rather on the hope of an afterlife, as recorded in tombs and mummies. There are also the hieroglyphs – pictorial writing that seems to promise so much more than a simple alphabet. And there is the ancient Egyptian religion itself, with its variety of transcendental beings, ranging from the mightiest of demiurges to the most localised of spirits.

Gods were closely allied to human life in ancient Egypt. The high gods, those with whom the kings identified themselves, represented just about every form of psychic power. The Sun-god Re ruled over the other gods and mankind, and the Egyptian king called himself 'Son of Re'. Other gods, who started as local deities, joined with Re in compromise rather than in struggle. So Amun of Thebes became Amun-Re, and the priests of Ptah of Memphis explained that Re was his father as he, in turn, was the father of other gods.

In myths telling of the creation, the sky and the earth gave birth to other gods, namely Seth and Osiris, and to the goddesses Isis and Nephthys. Osiris, who was the god of fertility and of resurrection in the other world, became the most important god of all. His wife, Isis, gave birth to Horus; and with Nephthys, whose husband was supposed to

be Seth, Osiris went on to father Anubis, known as the god of death.

Osiris was good and bountiful. He taught the Egyptians to till and to cultivate the fields, also providing them with law and religion. Seth, however, succumbed to jealousy and laid plans to kill him. Seth tracked down and dismembered Osiris, scattering his body across Egypt, but Isis was able to collect the parts together, bandaging them into what is said to have been the first mummy, and breathing life into him once more. Horus, the child they then conceived, went on to contend with Seth. A memorial tablet left by one king of Egypt told of his knowledge of the god:

'Your nature, Osiris, is more secret than other gods. You become young according to your own wish. You appear in order to dispel darkness, for the gods and magic come into existence to illuminate your majesty and bring your enemies to shambles.'

Lower gods in ancient Egypt concerned themselves with everyday affairs, however. One of the

In the statue of Osiris, above, the crook and flail represent his role as inaugurator of Egyptian agriculture. These symbols are also used in today's occult regalia.

In the statue, right, Isis suckles Horus. The 'madonna-and-child' played an important part in the resurrection-based Osirian religion.

The Egyptian Sun-god Re, seen left with the head of a falcon, rides in his boat across the sky, bringing light to the world. On his head he carries a solar disk representing the Sun. Re was often identified with the falcon-headed sky god Horus, whose eyes, many believed, were the Sun and the Moon.

Thoueris (or Ta-urt), the Egyptian goddess of childbirth, below, was often represented as a hippopotamus standing on its hind legs.

oldest of the Egyptian deities, Thoueris or Ta-urt, was goddess of pregnancy and birth. Any woman in Egypt might pray to her statue or wear an amulet that showed the goddess as a hippopotamus standing on its hind legs. The god Bes became husband to Thoueris; and he, too, despite a fearsome appearance, was a friend to all.

HOLY CONSULTATIONS

People sought out 'consultations' with these gods in ways that link with forms of fortune-telling and dream interpretation in use today. Someone seeking advice might spend the night in a temple courtyard in the hope that the god would appear in a dream. Indeed, attendants, magicians and dream interpreters thronged the temples to offer their

help. One formula that was guaranteed to produce a vision of the god Bes involved, first, writing out a petition with an ink that included ingredients such as the blood of a white dove. Then:

'Make a drawing of the god on your left hand and wrap your hand in a strip of black cloth that has been consecrated to Isis and lie down to sleep without speaking a word, even in answer to a question.'

Much of the impact that ancient Egyptian society has had on the modern imagination stems from the massive accumulation of material associated with tombs and mummies. The ancient Egyptians believed that life could continue after death. To ensure that this would happen, they provided the dead person with an illustrated guide, the so-called *Book of the Dead,* which might be inscribed on a papyrus left with the body or painted on the coffin or a wall of the tomb. The *Book of the Dead* shows the tests through which a spirit must go before merging with Osiris in everlasting life. It gives, with detailed precision, the responses that a spirit must

The union of Geb, god of the Earth, with Nut, goddess of the sky, which is said to have resulted in the births of Osiris, Isis, Seth and Nephthys, is depicted right.

make to persuade the gods to give judgement in its favour. The drawings – of scenes such as the 'weighing of the heart', and of gods and of creatures, such as the dreadful beast Amemt, who waited to devour the heart that was found wanting – have provided a starting point from which many artists, among them Austin Osman Spare, painting earlier this century, have derived symbolic motifs.

Egyptian mummies have always fascinated travellers from other countries. In medieval times, Arab physicians decided that ground-down mummy made a useful remedy for many ills. This belief passed to Europe; and in the 16th and 17th centuries, speculators shipped out vast quantities of 'physic'. During the 19th century, public unwrappings of mummies became a popular entertainment – even an archbishop of Canterbury was once turned away from a lecture hall that was packed to capacity. In 1827, just 10 years after Mary Wollstonecraft Shelley had written *Frankenstein*, Jane Webb published *The Mummy*. At the high spot of the action, two of the characters climb into the Great Pyramid, carrying with them a galvanic battery, and literally shock the mummy of King Cheops back into life.

'A fearful peal of thunder rolled in lengthened vibrations as the mummy rose slowly from its tomb. Edric saw the mummy stretch out its withered hand as though to seize him. He felt its tremendous grip. Then all was darkness... '

This fantasy has become the source of many film plots, from *The Mummy*, with Boris Karloff, in 1932, to *The Awakening*, with Charlton Heston, in 1980 – to say nothing of *Abbott and Costello Meet the Mummy* in 1954.

Later ages made their own interpretations – and misinterpretations – of the realities of ancient Egypt. The Greeks and the Romans, who dominated the country in the few hundred years just before and after the time of Christ, already thought of Egypt as a land of inexplicable mysteries. When the Arabs conquered Egypt, they spun wondrous tales about the riches and powers that the ancient kings had once possessed. They told of caskets piled high with sacred symbols made of gold, weapons

fashioned out of iron that could not rust, glass that could be bent without breaking, books made of leaves of gold that contained the history of the past and prophecies of the future.

OBELISKS AND SPHINXES

As Europeans began to travel to Egypt, increasing amounts of titillating information trickled back to the West, and by the 18th century Egyptiana had been taken up by the fashionable as part of the general enchantment with Classicism. Artists inserted pyramids, obelisks and sphinxes into their fantastic landscapes. Sir Isaac Newton dreamed up a new chronology for Egyptian history while trying to synchronise the list of Egyptian kings with the eras of biblical history. A French writer, Jean Terrasson, collected together all the extant Greek and Roman descriptions of Egypt and turned them into a vast novel, *The Life of Sethos*. Others pondered on the significance of hieroglyphs, assigning meanings to them according to arbitrary whims. For instance, Thomas Greenhill, a London surgeon, confidently proclaimed in 1705, in a book subtitled *On the Art of Embalming*, that the crocodile was the emblem of malice; the eye, the preserver of

Fantastic stories of the resurrection of ancient Egyptian mummies all derive from Jane Webb's The Mummy of 1827. The tale has since become a fertile source for horror films, offering title roles to numerous actors including Lon Chaney Jr in The Mummy's Curse, below left, and Christopher Lee in The Mummy, below.

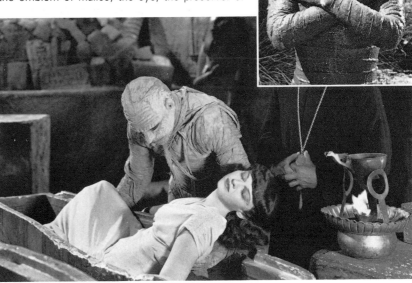

justice; and that the right hand, with its open fingers, signified plenty.

But such speculation was suddenly given a solid basis of fact after Napoleon invaded Egypt in 1798. A detachment of soldiers working on some fortifications near the coastal town of Rosetta turned up a slab of basalt carrying an inscription in Greek, as well as hieroglyphs and a demotic script that was a simplified form of Egyptian writing. Scholars could now work out how to read the hieroglyphs, although the task of deciphering them fully was to take another 20 years.

WIDESPREAD INFLUENCE

From then on, interest in Egypt grew and grew. Some travelled to Egypt to study its ancient civilisation. Others went to plunder as many antiquities as they could. Europe thus gradually became familiar with the temples and pyramids, the giant statues and the evocative script. The influence of ancient Egypt also showed up in areas such as furniture design: the Egyptian motif became part of both the Empire and the Regency styles, lingering on into Art Nouveau. Egyptian temples even provided the model for buildings, such as cotton mills in the north of England. Obelisks found their way to Europe and the United States. Organisations such as the Egypt Exploration Fund, founded in 1882, made Egyptological research generally available, and a burgeoning coterie of mystics incorporated all such information into their magical systems.

H. Rider Haggard, writing in the 1880s, also drew on the fashionable Egyptian hieroglyphs and burial places, embalmings and resurrections for his books *Cleopatra* and *She*, the story of Ayesha (She who-must-be-obeyed), a doomed love affair spreading across millennia.

Aleister Crowley, meanwhile, reached the conclusion that the true source of all wisdom was Seth,

Two potent symbols used in Egyptian amulets as a protection against evil were the Eye of Horus, below, and the ankh, bottom, a key-like cross that represented life. Both of these symbols are incorporated into several modern occult ceremonials.

later worshipped as Satan. Seth, he claimed, had appeared to him while he was in Cairo in 1904, in the form of a bodiless intelligence named Aiwass, and had dictated to him the three chapters that make up *The Book of the Law*. This is the book that expounds the basic Crowleyian principle. As Crowley put it: '"Do what thou wilt" shall be the whole of the Law.'

In Egypt, Aleister Crowley, who would later refer to his string of mistresses as the 'Apes of Thoth', looked for revelations in the Cairo Museum. He proudly regarded himself as the Beast of the Revelation, with the number 666 (see *The Book of Revelation* 13). Now, exhibit 666 in the Cairo museum happened to be a painted tablet commemorating an Egyptian priest, Ankh-f-nKhonsu. Crowley immediately decided that he had been Ankh-f-n-Khonsu in a previous life. He was also convinced

Leila Waddell, left, was one of Aleister Crowley's string of mistresses and magical assistants who were collectively known as the 'Apes of Thoth'. Crowley's burning ambition was to find one who was such an accomplished medium that he could contact his guardian angel through her.

that a new Age of Horus was about to replace the passing Age of Osiris with its resurrection-based Christian faith.

Fascination with Ancient Egypt persists. To take just one example, the Egyptians were given to wearing protective amulets, the most symbolically impressive being the Eye of Horus; and even today, a bracelet of lucky charms may well carry a distant relation, a tiny symbol of an *ankh* (a key-like cross), the Egyptian sign for life.

▟▌ THE CROWLEYS TOOK A FLAT IN CAIRO AND CROWLEY TRIED TO CONJURE UP SYLPHS (SPIRITS OF THE AIR) . . . AT MIDNIGHT, HE MADE THE INVOCATION ACCORDING TO HIS WIFE'S INSTRUCTIONS... AND WAS TOLD THROUGH HER THAT... A NEW EPOCH IN HUMAN HISTORY HAD BEGUN AND THAT HE WAS TO FORM A LINK BETWEEN SOLAR-SPIRITUAL FORCES AND MANKIND. ▟▌

COLIN WILSON, ALEISTER CROWLEY: THE NATURE OF THE BEAST

ALEISTER CROWLEY, ONE OF THE MOST INFAMOUS ENGLISHMEN OF THE 20TH CENTURY, HAD MANY INTERESTS, AMONG THEM MOUNTAINEERING, DRUGS, PORNOGRAPHY – AND 'MAGICK'. HE EVEN BELIEVED THAT HE WAS THE 'BEAST' OF THE BOOK OF REVELATION

In the late 20th century, psychical researchers, also known as parapsychologists, largely concern themselves with mental phenomena, such as telepathy and precognition. But however important the scientific implications of such supposed phenomena, there can be no doubt that they are less spectacular than the alleged physical phenomena of mediumship – such things as levitation and materialisations of departed spirits – which were the main focus of psychic investigations during the period 1860 to 1930.

At that time, there were many physical mediums, among whom the most notable, apart from

'THE WICKEDEST MAN IN THE WORLD'

the great D.D. Home, was Eusapia Palladino, an Italian medium whose powers impressed such serious researchers as Everard Feilding and Hereward Carrington.

But one amateur investigator in particular was not at all impressed by her. After a sitting with Palladino, he even came to the conclusion that she was no more than a clever illusionist and that all those who had recorded her supernatural feats, notably the extrusion of a phantom 'ectoplasm' limb, had been duped.

The seance in question took place in 1913, and the researcher was trying to answer one crucial question that had presented itself to his mind: 'Feilding and the rest are clever, wary, experienced and critical, but even so, can I be sure that, when they describe what occurs, they are dependable witnesses?'

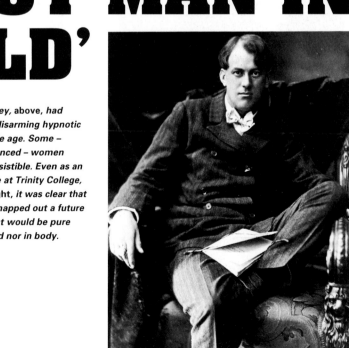

Aleister Crowley, above, had perfected his disarming hypnotic stare by middle age. Some – usually unbalanced – women found him irresistible. Even as an undergraduate at Trinity College, Cambridge, right, it was clear that Crowley had mapped out a future for himself that would be pure neither in mind nor in body.

Palladino sat at the end of a table – at her back, a curtained cabinet containing a stand on which were placed the various objects intended to be manipulated by her ghostly arm. Her right wrist was gripped by Mary d'Este Sturges; her left, by the investigator who had arranged the sitting.

The seance began in a way typical of many Palladino sittings: the curtain over the cabinet first bulged and then fell across the medium's left arm and hand and the investigator's right hand and arm. He reasoned to himself that this could not be the medium's left arm as he himself was holding it; but, as the mysterious arm disappeared from view, he suddenly felt Palladino's wrist slipping into his hand, although he had never been conscious of it ever leaving his grasp.

This minor but significant incident led the researcher to discount all the reports given by others who had attended Palladino's seances. 'If I,' he argued, '. . . cannot be relied upon to say whether I am or not holding a woman's wrist, is it not possible that even experts, admittedly excited by the rapidity with which one startling phenomenon succeeds another, may deceive themselves as to the conditions of the control?'

This investigator went on to have sittings with other mediums and to study the findings of other psychical researchers. As a result he became a complete sceptic, deciding that almost all the reported phenomena of the seance room were the outcome of fraud and self-deception.

DEDICATED OCCULTIST

Yet it is perhaps surprising that this particular investigator came to such negative conclusions. For, far from being a pure materialist, he was himself a dedicated occultist – none other, in fact, than Aleister Crowley, the practising ritual magician who, in the 1920s, was denounced as 'the wickedest man in the world'. His combination of total disbelief in

Jan: 10th 1910

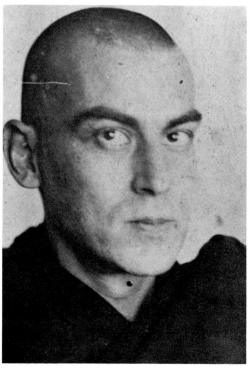

Crowley's marriage ('a detestable institution' he called it later) to Rose Kelly, a clergyman's daughter with whom he is seen above, was apparently perfectly happy until he discovered she was a dipsomaniac. After his divorce, he called all his mistresses 'Scarlet Women'.

Allan Bennett, left, was one of the few men whom Crowley revered, describing his mind as being 'pure, piercing and profound beyond any other'. Bennett taught Crowley magic when they were both members of the Order of the Golden Dawn. But they took different paths: Bennett went to Ceylon (now Sri Lanka) and became a Buddhist monk; Crowley became 'the Beast'.

Spiritualist mediumship with total belief in ritual magic was typical of the man: indeed, a thread of ambivalence and paradox ran right through his life, his teachings and his relationship with others.

Edward Alexander Crowley – later, he used only his first name, and adapted it to the unusual spelling of 'Aleister' – was born in October 1875. His parents were members of the Plymouth Brethren, that most strict of Protestant sects, and they brought up their only son in all its rigid belief – that every word of *The Bible* was the literal truth, inspired by the Holy Spirit, that the Catholic and

❚❚ EVERY MAN SHOULD MAKE MAGICK THE KEYNOTE OF HIS LIFE. HE SHOULD LEARN ITS LAWS AND LIVE BY THEM. ❚❚

ALEISTER CROWLEY,

MAGICK IN THEORY AND PRACTICE

_In_Focus

SEX MAGICK

Crowley's pornographic treatise on mysticism, _The Scented Garden_, was an early reflection of what were to become his two principal obsessions in life: 'magick' and sexual indulgence.

It was in Paris, at the end of 1913, that he first experimented with a series of rituals that involved the painting of a pentacle (in the attempt to invoke the god Mercury), a ritual dance performed by neophyte Victor Benjamin Neuburg, whom he had met in Cambridge, and the scourging of Neuburg's buttocks, as well as the cutting of a cross on the skin above his heart. Finally, an act of buggery was committed by the two men.

On one occasion, Neuburg apparently became so possessed that he thought Mercury had told them they should perform the ultimate act of sex magick by raping and murdering a woman, subsequently cutting her corpse into pieces, and then offering them as sacrifices. The prospect of such behaviour was too much even for Crowley, and the ceremony is said never to have been performed.

Apologists for Crowley maintain, however, that magick was never an excuse for sexual activity as far as he was concerned. Rather, they say, Crowley seems to have reached the conclusion that, like magick, sex requires a great deal of discipline and experimentation if great heights are to be reached, and can be used in the practice of magick.

Magick, too, could be used to win a lover, according to Crowley. As he wrote in _Magic in Theory and Practice:_ 'Suppose that I wish to win a woman who dislikes me and loves someone else. I have only to make my mind the master of hers... her mind will then present its recantation to her Will, her Will repeal its decision, and her body submit to mine as the seal of her surrender. Here the Magical Link exists... I may work naturally by wooing of course. But, magically, I may attack her astrally so that her aura becomes uneasy, responding no longer to her lover.'

Anglican Churches were 'synagogues of Satan', and that the overwhelming majority of mankind was doomed by a just God to roast in hellfire.

The elder Crowley died in 1887, and Aleister then became the object of his mother's fanatical venom. On more than one occasion, she accused him of being the actual 'Great Beast' of the _Book of Revelation,_ whose number is said to be 666. To the end of his life, Crowley did everything he could to live up to this archetypal image. Some say he even came to believe he really was the biblical Beast.

Sent away to a school for the sons of Brethren, he had many experiences that made him lose his Christian faith. He even acquired a hatred of the Brethren and their beliefs that was to survive throughout his long and eventful life.

In October.1895, Crowley, in possession of a fortune of £30,000 that he had inherited on reaching the age of 21 – became a student of Trinity College, Cambridge. His three years at the university were happy ones: he collected rare books, wrote much poetry, spent his holidays climbing in the Alps – and became interested in the occult.

This led him, in 1898, to become a Neophyte – a student member – of the Hermetic Order of the Golden Dawn, a semi-secret society devoted to the study of the occult arts and sciences, including the evocation of spirits, divination, and alchemy.

Aleister Crowley considered most of his fellow members of the Golden Dawn to be 'absolute nonentities'; but he was impressed by the occult

Despite some of the more ludicrous poses he affected, such as the one **right**, the core of Crowley's 'magick' seemed to be genuine enough. His famous, and much misunderstood, 'Do what thou wilt shall be the whole of the law' was amplified by 'Love is the law; love under will'. He constantly urged his followers to seek their true selves. This, he believed, was the divine purpose of all human lives. He may have taken the idea from the Elizabethan magician, Dr Dee, who had written: 'Do that which most pleaseth you... ' The unenlightened took this to advocate moral laxity; and in his less noble moments, so did Aleister Crowley.

magical abilities of two of them, Cecil Jones and Allan Bennett. The latter took up residence with Crowley in his London flat, and together the two carried out many occult experiments. Among these was the 'consecration' – the charging with magical powers – of a talisman intended to cure a certain Lady Hall of a serious illness.

This was duly prepared and handed over. Unfortunately, however, neither Lady Hall nor her daughter followed Crowley's precise instructions. So that when the talisman was applied to the venerable old lady, she was seized with a violent series of fits and nearly died.

The consecration that produced these unpleasant effects was probably carried out in what Crowley called the White Temple, a room lined with mirrors and devoted to white magic. But his flat also included another room, the Black Temple, in which the altar was supported by the image of a black man standing on his hands and which contained a skeleton to which it is said that Crowley would sacrifice sparrows.

INVISIBLE VANDALS

There seems to have been a thoroughly sinister atmosphere about Crowley's flat. One evening in 1899, he and a friend, also an occultist, went out to dinner. On their return, they found that the locked door of the White Temple had been mysteriously opened, its furniture overturned, and the 'magical symbols' that it held scattered around the room. As Crowley and his friend restored the room to order, they claimed clairvoyantly to have observed 'semi-materialised beings... marching around the main room in almost unending procession'.

In 1900, the Golden Dawn split into two competing factions. Crowley managed to quarrel with both of them; and for the next three years or so, he lost interest in western occultism. Instead, he wrote poetry, travelled the world and got married to a lady whom he called 'Ouarda the Seer', although she

actually knew little about the occult and probably cared even less about it.

In March 1904, the two were staying in Cairo. Crowley, wanting to demonstrate his occult abilities to his wife, carried out a number of magical rites. The results, if Crowley's written records are to be believed, were startling. He received a psychic message, flashed into his brain from some unknown source, which told him that a new epoch in history was about to begin. He, Crowley, had been chosen to be the prophet of this new age. Crowley's wife also received a message: that her husband was to sit down for one hour on three consecutive days with a pen and paper before him. The gods would then dictate to him, in voices audible only to their chosen prophet, the gospel of the new age that was to dawn.

Crowley obeyed the directions. He heard a voice, presumably originating in the depths of his own mind, and wrote down the words dictated to him. The result was *The Book of the Law*, a prose poem which Crowley came to believe was inspired in precisely the same way that his parents had believed *The Bible* to be inspired.

The meaning of some parts of *The Book of the Law* is obscure. Even Crowley admitted that some passages were beyond his own comprehension. But the basic message was clear. Crowley was to be the prophet of a new era – the so-called Age of Horus. In the new age, all the old religions of mankind – Christianity, Islam and Buddhism, for instance – would pass away and be replaced by a new faith of 'Force and Fire', the basic moral principle of which would be complete self-fulfilment. 'Every man and woman is a star', Crowley was told – in other words, each individual has an absolute

right to develop in his or her own way. 'Do what thou wilt shall be the whole of the law', said the new gospel, for 'Thou hast no right but to do thy will' and 'The word of sin is restriction'.

 DO WHAT THOU WILT SHALL BE THE WHOLE OF THE LAW, SAID THE NEW GOSPEL, FOR THOU HAST NO RIGHT BUT TO DO THY WILL AND THE WORD OF SIN IS RESTRICTION.

In fairness to Crowley and his followers, it has to be emphasised that he was always careful to point out that 'Do what thou wilt' is not quite the same as 'Do what you like'. When *The Book of the Law* says 'Do what thou wilt', claimed Crowley, it means 'Find the way of life that is in accordance with your inmost nature and then live it to the full.'

For some years, Crowley only half-believed in the truth and importance of *The Book of the Law*, but by 1910 it had mastered him, and he devoted the rest of his life to spreading its message and converting others to the belief that he, Aleister Crowley, was a new messiah.

The methods he adopted to achieve these ends included the authorship of numerous books, most of them eventually published at the expense of himself and his followers, the setting up of two occult fraternities, the public performance of occult ceremonies at London's Caxton Hall, and even the establishment of an 'Abbey', situated in a derelict Sicilian farmhouse, the inmates of which devoted themselves to the practices of the new faith.

Leila Waddell, violinist and Crowley's magical assistant in London in 1910, is seen left. She played the violin in Crowley's Rites of Eleusis at Caxton Hall, which was open to the public. Crowley claimed magically to have changed her from being 'a fifth-rate fiddler' to a musical genius – but just for the evening.

Crowley and his 'Scarlet Woman' Leah Hirsig, pose, right, with their baby, Poupée, outside the infamous Abbey of Thelema in Sicily in 1921. An experiment in communal living for students of 'magick', the Abbey was a disaster from the first, ending in 1923 with the death of one of its members.

Jane Wolfe (left in the picture, far right), a former stage and screen actress, is seen with Leah Hirsig outside the Abbey in 1921. The centre attracted many visitors from all over the world. Some were horrified (especially when Crowley offered them 'cakes of light', which were made of dung; and most went away utterly disappointed.

A sketch by Crowley of a devouring demon is shown above.

'The Devil', right, is from a Tarot pack, designed by Crowley and painted by Lady Frieda Harris. The work on the cards was expected to take three months, but it eventually took all of five years.

In the years before the outbreak of the First World War, Crowley and a few disciples carried out an intensive propaganda campaign in England. This, although it cost all of Crowley's money and much of that belonging to his friends, was notably unsuccessful. Few converts were made, and Crowley was subjected to much unfavourable publicity. In 1914, Crowley took himself and his new faith to the United States where, so he hoped, people would be more receptive to the new gospel and to his 'magick' – the occult system Crowley derived from his synthesis of western occultism, the teachings contained in *The Book of the Law,* and the tantrism (yogic theory and practice, largely concerned with sexuality) that he had learned from eastern sources.

But the New World proved even more resistant to Crowley's influence than the Old. The six years the self-proclaimed prophet spent in America were unhappy. He was perpetually short of money, made few converts, and was accused of being a traitor to his own country – reasonably enough for, until the United States' entry into the war in 1917, he earned a scanty living by editing a pro-German propaganda sheet.

In 1920, he returned to Europe along with two mistresses – Crowley always maintained a vigorous sex life – and established his 'Abbey of Thelema'

The pornographic wall painting, above, is from the Abbey of Thelema – one of the lesser of its evils, according to reports in the world's press.

(a magical word, implying 'New Aeon', though Crowley often translated it as 'will') in Sicily. For a time, this enjoyed a modest success. The Sicilians were surprisingly tolerant of Crowley and his 'magick', and a number of disciples, actual and potential, made their way to the Abbey. These included Jane Wolfe, a minor Hollywood star, Norman Mudd, a one-eyed professor of mathematics, and Raoul Loveday, a brilliant young Oxford graduate who had decided to devote his life to Crowley's new religion.

Loveday died while he was staying at the Abbey, probably of enteritis. His wife, who believed that her husband had been poisoned by blood that he had drunk in the course of an occult ceremony, returned to London and began a virulent newspaper campaign against Crowley. Eventually, this campaign, which included the denunciation of Crowley as 'a beast in human form', led to the closure of the Abbey. The Sicilian authorities then promptly deported him.

The remainder of Crowley's life was, in many ways, an anti-climax. He wandered through Europe, a lonely and increasingly unhappy man, and eventually died in 1947. At the time of his death, Crowley had only a handful of followers: today, however, he has many thousands. In some ways, his teachings seem more in tune with the present than they were with his own times.

WERE THE NAZIS BLACK MAGICIANS?

WAS THE TERRIFYING HOLD OF THE NAZI LEADERSHIP DUE TO FEAR ALONE, OR DID THEY ACTUALLY ENGAGE IN THE USE OF OCCULT POWERS TO THIS END?

The goal of every magician is power over natural forces. He aims to seize the infinite forces of the cosmos and wield them, like a sword, in his own service. A magician who seeks this power for his own ends, without the wish to serve any higher good, is known as a black magician; and, according to most magical schools of thought, he pays a high price in the end for such pride. Often, he becomes possessed by the spirits he calls upon and is destroyed by them. In the view of several occultists, Adolf Hitler was just such a

Karl Dönitz, below, commander of the U-boat fleet, met Hitler as infrequently as possible because he felt the Führer's 'powers of suggestion' impaired his judgement as an individual.

powerful black magician. Indeed, according to one of Hitler's few friends from his early years in Linz, his personal power had developed by the time he was 15 years old, and very startling it was. On one occasion, his former friend recalled:

'Adolf Hitler stood in front of me and gripped my hands and held them tight... The words did not come smoothly from his mouth as they usually did, but rather erupted, hoarse and raucous... It was as if another being spoke out of his body and moved him as much as it moved me. It was not at all a case of a speaker carried away by his own words. On the contrary, I rather felt as though he himself listened with astonishment and emotion to what burst forth from him with elemental force...'

This friend was August Kubizek, and he was describing a midnight walk, in 1904, with the 15-year-old Hitler following a performance of Wagner's opera *Rienzi*, which tells the story of the meteoric rise and fall of a Roman tribune. Hitler's emotional speech concerned the future of Germany and 'a mandate which, one day, he would receive from the people to lead them from servitude...'

According to Kubizek, Hitler spent a great deal of time studying oriental mysticism, astrology, hypnotism, Germanic mythology and other aspects of occultism. By 1909, he had made contact with Dr Jörg Lanz von Liebenfels, a former Cistercian monk who, two years previously, had opened a temple of the 'Order of New Templars' at the tumbledown Werfenstein Castle, near Grein in Austria.

Born plain Adolf Lanz, von Liebenfels had actually assumed his aristocratic-sounding name.

His following was small but wealthy. An enthusiastic disciple of Guido von List – the 19th century leader of a neo-pagan movement who had adopted the swastika (originally a symbol of good luck) as his emblem – Lanz flew a swastika flag from his battlements – is said to have performed ritual magic and also ran a magazine that was entitled *Ostura*, a propaganda journal of occultism and race mysticism, to which the young Hitler was become an avid subscriber. In 1932, von Liebenfels wrote about the future Führer to a colleague:

'Hitler is one of our pupils . . . you will one day experience that he, and through him we, will one day be victorious and develop a movement that will make the world tremble.'

One of von Liebenfels' pronouncements was that human breeding farms should be set up 'in order to eradicate Slavic and Alpine elements from Germanic heredity', prefiguring Himmler's idea of an SS stud farm by over 20 years.

By the onset of the First World War, Hitler seems to have developed an unshakable conviction of his own high destiny. Indeed, as a messenger at the front, he took enormous risks, as if he knew that fate would not allow him to die just yet. And by the time the war ended, he had developed that curious, impersonal power over all those around him that was to stand him in such good stead.

Again and again, the idea that Hitler was in some way 'possessed' is to be found echoed in the writings of those who knew him. His uncanny hold over individuals was a bugbear to those in the highest echelons of the state. Once, for example, Dr Hjalmar Schacht – Hitler's financial wizard – asked Hermann Göring to speak to Hitler about a minor point of economic policy. But, in Hitler's presence, Göring found himself unable to raise the matter. As he told Schacht: 'I often make up my mind to say something to him, but when I meet him face to face, my heart sinks... '

Grand Admiral Karl Dönitz was so conscious of the Führer's influence that he even avoided his company altogether so as to leave his own judgement unimpaired. As he put it:

'I purposely went very seldom to his headquarters, for I had the feeling that I would best preserve my power of initiative and also because, after several days at headquarters, I always had the feeling

The Italian dictator Benito Mussolini – seen below in civilian clothes – visited Hitler in Germany in 1943, mentally exhausted and deeply depressed. Yet Hitler's influence and the force of his personality were so strong that, according to Josef Goebbels, after only four days in Hitler's company, Mussolini underwent a complete transformation.

The children playing above came from the Steinhöring Lebensborn, one of many SS breeding farms set up by Heinrich Himmler in order to ensure the production of a Nordic 'super race'.

Hitler's ability to mesmerise individuals and groups – as at the informal gathering of his followers in Munich in the mid-1930s, left – led many to believe that he had supernatural powers.

that I had to disengage myself from his powers of suggestion... I was doubtless more fortunate than his staff, who were constantly exposed to his power and personality.'

FORCE OF PERSONALITY

In his diary for 7 April 1943, Josef Goebbels recorded a remarkable instance of Hitler's use of the force of his personality. The Italian dictator Mussolini had visited Germany in a state of deep depression and mental exhaustion. But, as Goebbels wrote:

'By putting every ounce of nervous energy into the effort, he [Hitler] succeeded in pushing Mussolini back onto the rails. In those four days, the Duce underwent a complete change. When he got out of the train on his arrival, the Führer thought he looked like a broken old man. When he left again, he was in high fettle, ready for anything.'

In March 1936, Hitler made a statement that precisely summed up the impressions of those who knew him best: 'I am going the way Providence dictates,' he said, 'with the assurance of a sleepwalker.' It was as if something else – not his own mind and soul – was in charge of his every action.

But this ruling spirit, if such it was, proved not always kind to its host. Hitler's frantic, screaming rages – when he would literally froth at the mouth and fall to the floor – are well-documented. Even more frightening is the account given by his confidant Hermann Rauschning in his book *Hitler Speaks*:

'He wakes up in the night, screaming and in convulsions. He calls for help, and appears to be half paralysed. He is seized with panic that makes him tremble until the bed shakes. He utters confused and unintelligible sounds, gasping as if on the point of suffocation.'

Hitler was not certain at all times of his 'guiding spirit's' intentions, and suffered from a horror of ill omens. Albert Speer, who became his personal architect and finally Germany's Minister of War Production, recounted an incident in October 1933 that shook Hitler's confidence more than anything so far. Laying the foundation stone of the House of German Art in Munich, which had been designed by his friend Paul Ludwig Troost and which Hitler felt embodied the highest ideals of Teutonic architecture, the Führer tapped the stone with a silver

hammer, only to find that it shattered to fragments in his hand. For almost three months, Hitler was wrapped in morbid gloom. Then, on 21 January 1934, Troost died. Hitler's relief was immediate. He told Speer: 'When that hammer shattered, I knew at once it was an evil omen. Something is going to happen, I thought. Now we know why the hammer broke. The architect was destined to die.'

SORCERER'S APPRENTICE

Josef Goebbels pretended to have an interest in the occult and astrology in order to please the Führer – even going so far as to gain proficiency in drawing up a horoscope. Rudolf Hess, Hitler's deputy, may also have dabbled to a degree in occult matters. But there was only ever one true 'sorcerer's apprentice' in Hitler's inner circle.

Heinrich Himmler was born of middle-class parents in Munich in 1900. A weak, pale and characterless youth, whose defective eyesight compelled him to wear thick-lensed spectacles, he became a fervent Nazi in the early 1920s and was appointed secretary to the Nazi Party propaganda office in Lower Bavaria. There, in his little office, he would sit and talk to a portrait of Hitler on the wall, long before he met the man himself. Although he had indubitable organising ability, Himmler's appearance made him something of a laughing stock, and it was almost jocularly that Hitler appointed him Deputy Reichsführer of the SS – the *Schutzstaffel*, or protective force, comprising about 300 men, dedicated to bodyguard duties.

But, by 1933, Himmler had built up the SS to such a strength that he was confident enough to purge it – retaining only men of the finest 'Germanic' physical characteristics and insisting that its officers should be able to prove a non-Jewish ancestry going back to 1750. After a lengthy, quasi-mystical induction, recruits were given a ceremonial dagger and permission to wear the full black uniform of the SS, complete with silver death's head. Thereafter, they were obliged to attend what Francis King, author of *Satan and the Swastika*, describes as 'neo-pagan ceremonies of a specifically SS religion devised by Himmler and clearly derived from his interest in occultism.'

Himmler had abandoned his Catholic faith for Spiritualism, astrology and mesmerism in his late teens. He was convinced that he was the reincarnation of Heinrich the Fowler, founder of the Saxon royal house, who died in 936. All these elements were incorporated into his SS 'religion'.

He even devised new festivals to take the place of such Christian events as Christmas and Easter, as well as special SS baptism and marriage ceremonies – though he believed polygamy would best serve the interests of the SS élite – and also issued instructions on the correct manner of committing suicide.

The centre of the SS 'cult' was to be found at the castle of Wewelsburg in Westphalia, which Himmler bought as a ruin in 1934 and went on to rebuild over the next 11 years at a cost of 13 million marks. The central banqueting hall contained a vast round table with 13 throne-like seats to accommodate Himmler and 12 of his closest 'apostles' – making, as some occult writers have pointed out, a coven of 13. Beneath this hall was a 'Hall of the Dead'. Here, plinths stood around a stone table. As each member of the inner circle of the SS died, his coat of arms would be burned and, together with his ashes, the remains would then be placed in an urn on one of these plinths for veneration.

In this slightly ludicrous theatrical atmosphere, Himmler instigated the systematic genocide carried out by the Third Reich in its last years. Millions of Jews, gypsies, homosexuals and others who did not conform to the ideals of the Führer, and of himself, were slaughtered. Many Nazi atrocities were in fact prompted by Himmler's bizarre theories. For example, his belief in the power of 'animal heat' led to experiments in which victims were exposed in freezing cold water and then revived – if they were fortunate – by being placed between the naked bodies of prostitutes. On another occasion, he decided

*In*Focus

RITUALS OF AN SS CASTLE

In August 1934, Reichsführer-SS Heinrich Himmler officially took possession of the Wewelsburg castle, near Paderborn in Westphalia, as a museum and college for the ideological education of SS officers. Himmler, however, had much greater plans for the place: he intended it to become the bastion of an SS order, similar to the awesome castle of Marienburg built by the medieval Teutonic knights. The man who fired Himmler's dream was Karl Maria Wiligut (1866-1946), a mystic who claimed to possess an ancestral-clairvoyant memory and esoteric knowledge of Germanic mythology.

Wiligut had been committed to an insane asylum in 1924 – his report diagnosed schizophrenia with megalomaniac paranoid delusions – and was released in 1927. Six years later, he joined the SS as an expert on prehistoric German history. In this capacity, he corresponded with Himmler, with whom he established a friendly relationship, on a variety of topics, including cosmology and runic wisdom. Above all, Wiligut predicted that the castle was destined to become a 'bastion' in an apocalyptic war against a vast army from the East.

Wilgut's ideas on religion and tradition also influenced the castle's commandant who introduced new rituals, such as pagan wedding ceremonies for SS officers and their brides. Wiligut officiated at these ceremonies and would hold an ivory-handled stick bound with blue ribbon and carved with runes. The castle also held annual spring, harvest and solstice festivals for the SS and local villagers. Himmler even asked Wiligut to design the SS death's head ring – the symbol of SS membership. The result comprised a death's head (a skull), Germanic runes (including the runic form of double 'S', which stood for victory and was used on SS collar badges), and the swastika.

that statistics should be collected of the measurements of Jewish skulls; but only the skulls of the newly dead were deemed suitable, so hundreds of people were decapitated to this end.

Less horrific but certainly strange, meanwhile, were SS researches into the suppression of the Irish harp in Ulster, the occult significance of Gothic towers and the Eton top hat, and the magical power of the bells of Oxford which, Himmler decided, had put a charm on the Luftwaffe, preventing it from inflicting serious damage on the city.

The occult writer J. H. Brennan has gone so far as to suggest that Himmler was a 'non-person', a zombie without mind or soul of its own, drawing power from Hitler like a psychic leech. And author Francis King has pointed out that the huge Nuremberg rallies, presided over by Hitler at his most possessed, fulfil the conditions necessary for what some witch cults describe as a 'cone of power': searchlights would pierce the night sky in a conical pattern above vast crowds, generating a giant surge of emotion, centred on the strutting figure of the Führer.

But if Himmler could be magically influenced for evil, he could also be influenced for good. The unlikely instrument of this good was a plump, blond masseur and occultist, Felix Kersten. He had been

The castle of Wewelsburg near Paderborn in north-west Germany, above, was bought by Heinrich Himmler, top, in 1934 and became the temple of his SS cult. The presence of a gypsy caravan so close to the Nazi shrine would not have been tolerated, for gypsies were among the millions of non-Aryans exterminated by Himmler in his attempt to 'purify' the Germanic race.

trained in osteopathy and allied skills by a mysterious Chinese doctor named Ko. Dr Ko was also an occultist and mystic, who apparently developed the latent psychic powers that Kersten possessed. Fame soon came to Kersten, and he was ordered to attend Himmler, who suffered from chronic stomach cramps, in 1938. Thereafter, the SS chief became almost totally dependent on Kersten, who was able, on a number of occasions, to save hundreds of Jewish lives by his hold on Himmler's mind. Indeed, a postwar investigating commission concluded that Kersten's service to mankind was 'so outstanding that no comparable precedent could be found for it in history.'

By what appears to have been sheer force of will, Kersten persuaded Himmler on more than one occasion to defer the extermination of concentration camp prisoners. Kersten would then keep on about the matter until Himmler dropped the whole business. He also managed, with at least partial success, to influence Himmler through deliberate misinterpretation of horoscopes – in which Himmler believed more fervently, perhaps, than Hitler.

From the middle of 1942, Kersten was busy sowing in Himmler's mind the notion that he should try to make a separate peace with the Western Allies. Yet, though he drew the Reichsführer to the

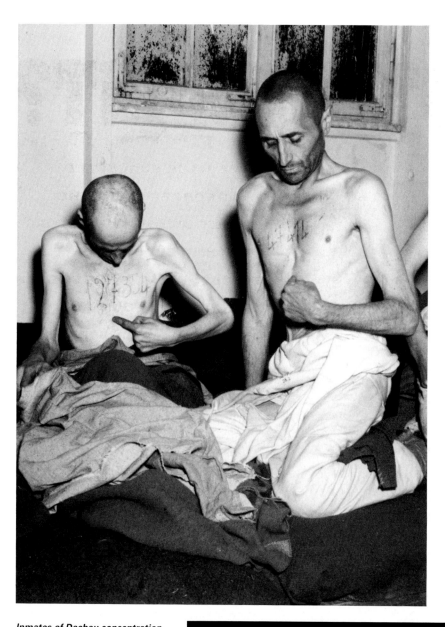

brink on several occasions, he was unable to counteract the awesome power wielded by Hitler.

As Francis King has pointed out, Hitler's policies, as Germany approached its collapse, tallied exactly with what could be expected of a black magician's pact with evil powers. The essence of such a pact lies in sacrifice – an orgy of blood and destruction.

'Losses,' Hitler told Field Marshal Walther von Reichenau, 'can never be too high. They sow the seeds of future greatness.' As the historian Hugh Trevor-Roper was to put it: 'Like an ancient hero, Hitler wished to be sent with human sacrifices to the grave.'

Hitler, although he knew all hope had gone, waited in his bunker until 30 April 1945 before shooting himself, with Eva Braun, whom he had just married. The date was too significant to occultists to be a coincidence. It was the day that ends in *Walpurgis* night – the high feast of the powers of darkness.

// ALLIANCES COULD BE FORMED WITH THE MASTER OF THE WORLD OR THE KING OF FEAR... THOSE WHO CONCLUDE A PACT WILL CHANGE THE SURFACE OF THE EARTH AND ENDOW THE HUMAN ADVENTURE WITH A NEW MEANING FOR MANY THOUSANDS OF YEARS... **//**

LOUIS PAUWELS AND JACQUES BERGIER, THE MORNING OF THE MAGICIANS

Inmates of Dachau concentration camp point to the serial numbers scratched on their chests, above, on liberation in 1945 by the U.S. Seventh Army. Prisoners such as these Jews were used by the Third Reich for a whole series of bizarre and cruel experiments, which few survived.

PERSPECTIVES

FALSE LINKS?

The idea that the Nazis had strong links with the occult – and gained much of their power from demonic sources – has held a particular fascination with generations born after World War II. It is a theme that has complex roots, but many of the claims often made have no basis in fact. One of these concerns the importance of the nationalistic, anti-Semitic Thule Society, founded in Munich in 1912, whose emblem showed a long dagger that was superimposed on a shining swastika sun-wheel.

In *The Morning of the Magicians,* authors Louis Pauwels and Jacques Bergier claim that Adolf Hitler was deeply influenced in occult matters by two members of the Thule Society – Dietrich Eckart (1869-1923) and Karl Haushofer (1869-1946). According to the two authors, Thule was at one time the magic

centre of a vanished civilization, though not all its secrets had been lost. Members of the Thule Society, such as Eckart and Haushofer, were to inherit 'a reservoir of forces which would be drawn on to enable Germany to dominate the world.' These members are also said to have instilled the myths of Aryan supremacy 'into the mediumistic mind of Hitler.' Indeed, the Thule Society was to become the 'magic centre of the Nazi movement.'

In fact, the Thule Society was dissolved around 1925. Eckart, apparently, was never a member and no evidence exists to link Haushofer with the society. Nevertheless, another author, Dietrich Bronder, in his book *Bevor Hitler Kam* ('Before Hitler Came') also states – wrongly – that Hitler, Mussolini, Herman Hess and Himmler were members.

SATANIST OR SAINT?

SOME HAVE SUGGESTED THAT SORCERY WAS THE SECRET OF JOAN OF ARC'S UNCANNY SUCCESS IN BATTLE. WHAT EVIDENCE IS THERE FOR SUCH CLAIMS CONCERNING HER SUPPOSED PARANORMAL POWERS AND CLOSE INVOLVEMENT WITH THE BLACK ARTS?

J oan of Arc's enemies, the English, believed that she was a sorceress and a harlot, in league with the powers of darkness. There could, in their eyes, be no other reason to explain the ignominious defeats they had suffered at her hands. This English view of Joan – known both as the Maid of Orléans and *La Pucelle* (the Virgin) – was described 150 years after her death in Shakespeare's play *Henry VI, Part I*. In this, she is dragged away to the stake, begging for mercy. To escape the flames, she claims she is with child, naming first the Duke of Alençon and then the King of Naples as the father. When this ruse fails, her last act is to curse the Duke of York, who retorts:

'Break thou in pieces and consume to ashes
Thou foul accursed minister of hell!'

The suggestion that Joan had, in her last moments, claimed that she was pregnant in order to escape being burnt was a calumny of particular significance. Indeed, an important element in Joan's sexual mystique was her claim throughout her life that she was a virgin since, in the 15th century, it was a recognised fact that the Devil could have no dealings with a virgin.

Earlier in the same scene in Shakespeare's play, Joan speaks up for herself, maintaining that she is not only immaculate and chosen by God, but also of royal birth:

A quarter of a century after her death, Joan was formally exonerated; and almost 500 years later, in 1920, she was canonised. The stained glass window of St Joan, left, is in the chapel of Croft House School, Dorset, England.

Joan's birthplace, above, was near the church at Domrémy in Lorraine where, as a young girl, she began to hear 'voices'. One of these, Joan claimed, belonged to the archangel Michael, right. At Joan's trial, her voices were taken as evidence that she was a 'disciple of the fiend', as was her admission that, as a child, she had danced round the Fairies' Tree, said to be frequented by evil spirits and those who practised spells. Further evidence of her paranormal powers was the fact that she was able to tell Robert de Baudricourt in Vaucouleurs the outcome of the Battle of Herrings, below right, on 12 February 1429, on the very day it was fought 200 miles (320 kilometres) away near Orléans.

'First let me tell you whom you have condemn'd:
Not me begotten of a shepherd swain,
But issued from the progeny of kings:
Virtuous and holy, chosen from above
By inspiration of celestial grace,
To work exceeding miracles on earth.'

The play thus draws together two opposing views of Joan – one view that she was a witch and a whore, and her own view that she was the Virgin of God; and it gives a powerful impression of the confusion that surrounded her trial.

The result of her trial was a foregone conclusion. The English wanted her dead at all costs; and on 2 September 1430, they paid the colossal sum of 10,000 francs to her Burgundian captors for 'the purchase of Joan the Maid, who is said to be a sorcerer, a warlike person, leading the armies of the Dauphin.' Joan was a thorn in their side and one best removed as soon as possible. The justice that disposed of her was a 15th-century justice – vastly different from modern justice. As Edward Lucie-Smith points out in his *Joan of Arc:* 'The trial was merely to legitimise the burning.' Nevertheless, the case against Joan had to look good.

She was initially indicted on 70 counts, many of them charges of witchcraft and sorcery. But by the time the crucial stage of her trial was reached, the number of counts had been reduced to 12 and all references to witchcraft had been eliminated, save one. She was eventually condemned chiefly for her resistance to 'the Church on earth' – in essence, a theological crime.

The one remaining reference to witchcraft in the trial records concerned the 'Fairies' Tree', under which Joan had often played as a child. An account of her supposed involvement in strange ceremonies there appeared in the Acts of Accusation:

'Near the village of Domrémy stands a certain large and ancient tree, commonly called *l'arbre charmine faée de Bourlemont,* and near the tree is a fountain. It is said that round about live evil spirits, called fairies, with whom those who practise spells are wont to dance at night, wandering about the tree and the fountain. The said Joan was wont to

may genuinely have believed that Joan was a witch; the rank-and-file soldiers who had retreated before her in battle certainly thought she was one. Without the help of the Devil, so they reasoned, it would have been impossible for her to prevail against them. After Joan's relief of Orléans, the Duke of Bedford wrote to the English King Henry VI that the retreat from Orléans had been due to:

'A disciple and lyme of the fiend, called the Pucelle that used fals enchauntments and sorcerie, the which... nought oonly lessed... the nombre of your peuple there, but as well withdrowe the courage of the remenant, in marveilous wyse, and couraged your advers partie and enemy's.'

But apart from the Maid's uncanny success in battle, what other reasons were there to connect her with the black arts?

First and foremost, she did appear to be something of a seer. Indeed, her most controversial prophecy was foretelling the English victory at the so-called Battle of Herrings on 12 February 1429 at Rouvray, near Orléans. On that very day, Joan (hundreds of miles away at Vaucouleurs) told Robert de Baudricourt that the French had been heavily defeated; and when the news was confirmed two days later, Baudricourt took it as a sign that Joan was divinely inspired, sending her on her way to the Dauphin. In his book *Jeanne d'Arc,* W. S. Scott suggests that this knowledge might have been the result of precognitive vision.

There was also the matter of her psychic knowledge of the Dauphin's secret prayer. When Joan first met him at Chinon, he naturally enough needed to be convinced that this girl had indeed been sent by God to lead his armies. Joan is said to have been able to tell him about a secret prayer he had made – that if he were indeed the rightful ruler of France, God would defend him, or allow him to escape to Spain or Scotland in safety.

PSYCHIC DISCOVERY

Yet another strange event concerned the sword of Fierbois. While she was being equipped to join the Dauphin's armies, Joan said that her battle sword would be found buried behind the altar at St Catherine's Church at Fierbois. The sword was searched for and found, even though no one had known of the existence of any such sword. Joan thus seemed to have some inexplicable sixth sense, if not actual psychic powers.

Joan's refusal to repeat the Lord's Prayer at her trial was also taken as an indication that she was a witch. At that time, it was a common belief that no witch could say the Lord's Prayer without faltering: if Joan had inadvertently stumbled over the words, she might have seemed condemned out of her own mouth.

A dangerous ally for the Maid was the Franciscan friar, Brother Richard, whom she had first met at Troyes in July 1429. At her trial, she described how she countered his first overtures with some wit: 'When he came to me... he made the sign of the cross, and threw holy water, and I said to him: "Approach boldly – I will not fly away".'

Brother Richard was already a controversial figure for a series of sermons he had been preaching in Paris on the subject of the imminent coming of the Antichrist. Joan and he quickly established a

Joan's triumphal entry into Orléans, above, was painted by the French artist Jean Jacques Scherrer (1855-1916).

frequent the fountain and the tree, mostly at night, sometimes during the day; particularly, so as to be alone, at hours when in church the divine office was being celebrated. When dancing, she would turn around the tree and the fountain, then would hang on the boughs garlands of different herbs and flowers, made by her own hand, dancing and singing the while, before and after, certain songs and verses and invocations, spells, and evil arts. And the next morning, the chaplets of flowers would no longer be found there.'

But perhaps Joan herself, as she claimed in her defence, had taken the flowers away – or perhaps they just blew away. In any case, to hang a charge of witchcraft on a child's participation in what sounds like a country custom was ridiculous, even by 15th-century standards of justice.

Belief in, and the persecution of, witches was at its height in Europe at the time, and the English

religious rapport, and he became one of her confessors, as well as her standard-bearer at Charles' exhausting coronation. But he encouraged Joan in her deviations from religious orthodoxy, and made extravagant claims for her that did not help her image:

'[She] had as much power to know God's secrets as any saint in paradise... and... she could, if she wanted, make the King's army enter over the walls in any way she wanted.'

Eventually, there was a rift in their relationship, but the damage had been done: the sensational sermons and sorcerer's image tainted Joan's reputation to a marked degree.

Joan's trial from the 16th-century Armagnac manuscript is shown below. The trial lasted five months and was presided over by Pierre Cauchon, bishop of Beauvais (an English sympathiser) and Jean Le Maître, deputy inquisitor. After Joan had recanted of her supposed crimes, she was condemned to perpetual imprisonment; and when she relapsed, she was burnt at the stake.

The Maid's apparent lack of sexual identity also led to speculation as to whether she was in fact a girl. During her lifetime, Joan was examined three times to verify both her sex and her virginity: the evidence was that she was both female and *virgo intacta*. But, psychologically at least, she seemed to suffer from some confusion as to her sexual role. Her choice of male clothing was, she said, guided by her voices; but she certainly seemed to feel more comfortable in male dress. However, it also has to be said that dressing like a man encouraged her soldiers to think of her as a comrade in arms; and, certainly, it would have been uncomfortable for her to ride astride a horse in skirts.

FALSE MAIDS

Witch or not, Joan of Arc was condemned and, supposedly, burnt at the stake on 30 May 1431. But there is a theory that she escaped execution, and that a *bona fide* witch was burnt in her place. Several 'Joans' appeared in the years following her execution, the most convincing of whom was one who turned up in Orléans on 28 July 1439 and lodged there for a few days under the name of the Dame des Armoises. She received a payment for her past deeds on behalf of the city, and was apparently acknowledged by both Joan's brother and the king as the real Maid.

However, most contemporary chroniclers took the Dame des Armoises' claim with a pinch of salt; and in 1457, it was reported that she was released from prison 'having long called herself Jeanne la Pucelle, and deceived many persons who had seen Jeanne at the siege of Orléans.' She was never heard of again.

The false Joan fuelled speculation that the Maid might have been saved from the stake by order of the English regent, the Duke of Bedford, because she was of royal descent. Rumour had it that she was the illegitimate daughter of the promiscuous Queen Isabella (the Dauphin's mother) and Louis, Duke of Orléans. But unfortunately for this myth, the Duke had died years before Joan was born.

That a simple country girl should so seize the imagination of a monarch, an army and a people, and lead them to triumph is scarcely credible; but the knowledge of what really inspired Joan of Arc almost certainly perished with her in the fire.

" JOAN'S REFUSAL TO REPEAT THE LORD'S PRAYER AT HER TRIAL WAS ALSO TAKEN AS AN INDICATION THAT SHE WAS A WITCH... IT WAS A COMMON BELIEF THAT NO WITCH COULD SAY THE LORD'S PRAYER WITHOUT FALTERING: SO... SHE MIGHT HAVE SEEMED CONDEMNED OUT OF HER OWN MOUTH. **"**

In a scene from the film Saint Joan, *right, Joan (played by Jean Seberg) hears the sentence of the court. A friar (played by Kenneth Haigh) kneels beside her as she prays for strength.*

ALONGSIDE THE 'OFFICIAL' VIRGIN MARY EXISTS ANOTHER 'UNOFFICIAL' MADONNA – BLACK, MYSTERIOUS, ALL-POWERFUL AND POSSIBLY WITH RATHER DIFFERENT ORIGINS FROM HER CHASTE COUNTERPART

Until the late 18th century, pilgrims to Chartres, France, traditionally participated in a complex, intriguing and not unconventional Christian ritual. Having prayed in the abbey and heard mass in the cathedral, they would descend through a northern passageway to an ancient subterranean crypt beneath the church. Here, they would pay pious respects to *Notre Dame de Sous-Terre* (Our Lady of the Underworld) – a black ebony statue of a seated woman holding a child on her knees. On the statue's head, there was a crown: on its pedestal, a Roman inscription – *Virgini Paritures*

The Black Madonna, below, in the cathedral of Chartres, is the Virgin of the Pillar. The original stone column on which the figure stood is said to have been worn away by the bites and licks of its fervent worshippers.

(in translation, 'the Virgin who will give birth'). Having completed their devotions, pilgrims were then blessed with water drawn from a sacred well in the crypt. They were also permitted to drink of this water. Continuing their underground journey, they would at last emerge by a southern passage.

At the Benedictine monastery of Montserrat, in north-east Spain – where there is a particularly vigorous cult of the Virgin – a wooden statue of the Virgin and Child is also especially venerated. Indeed, Montserrat is a shrine for newly-weds, and the statue it contains is deemed to preside over marriage, sexuality and fertility. According to traditional legends, prayers to this statue are believed to ward off sterility.

Near Crotone, on a promontory overlooking the Gulf of Taranto in southern Italy, meanwhile, are the remains of a temple dedicated to Hera Lacinia, the Roman goddess of moonlight who protects women, especially in childbirth. She was believed to bring fertility and to govern the cycle of birth –

VIRGINS WITH A PAGAN PAST

The Polish Black Madonna, **left,** is known as Our Lady of Czestochwa. Like all Black Madonnas, she is accredited with supernatural powers and has thousands of enthusiastic followers.

conception, pregnancy, labour and delivery. Crotone's church, like Chartres and the monastery at Montserrat, houses a black statue of a woman. This statue, too, has become a magnet for pilgrims. On the second Sunday of May, she is carried from the cathedral at Crotone to the Church of Our Lady of Capo Colonne on the promontory. Then, by night, she is returned by sea in a procession of torchlit fishing boats – whose crews hope thereby to earn the statue's protection.

▮▮ ST BERNARD... EXPERIENCED HIS MOST DRAMATIC RELIGIOUS ILLUMINATION FROM THE BLACK MADONNA OF CHÂTILLON. WHILE HE WAS RECITING THE AVE MARIA BEFORE HER, SHE REPORTEDLY PRESSED HER BREAST, WHEREUPON MILK FELL INTO THE MONK'S OPEN MOUTH. **▮▮**

To the Roman Catholic Church as a whole, these three statues are officially regarded as Madonnas like any other, and no special status or significance is accorded them. But to the local people, and to the pilgrims who visit them, they have a significance and power that goes far beyond that accorded by the Catholic Church.

These statues are generally known as 'Black Madonnas'. In addition to the three already mentioned, there are at least 35 others, scattered not only throughout Europe, but as far away as Mexico. Among the most important of all the Black Madonna sites are Einsiedeln in Switzerland; Rocamadour, Dijon, Avioth and Le Puy in France; Orval in southern Belgium; and Loreto, Florence, Venice and Rome in Italy.

The statues, as their name suggests, are all black and are made of stone, ebony or Lebanese cedar. They are robed in sumptuously rich apparel and, on festive occasions, are often decked with precious stones. All of them are crowned. To their worshippers, they are the 'Queen of Heaven' and are attended by an image of the moon and/or stars – a belief that pre-dates Christianity and goes back to the pagan worship of female deities. All are depicted holding a child, usually on the left knee; all have become the object of pilgrimage; and all are believed to possess miraculous powers, especially of healing and fertility. The older ones have a curiously Middle-Eastern quality, possibly Byzantine or Egyptian. Many, like the one at Chartres, were destroyed during the French Revolution. Others, especially during the last 150 years, were officially replaced by more conventional statues of the Virgin – statues which are not black. Many of the original Black Madonnas have, over the centuries, even been purposely painted over with whitewash.

Black Madonnas are surrounded by legend and many are said to have appeared in miraculous circumstances. The Black Madonna at Tindari, Sicily, for example, is said to have been washed ashore in a casket. At Loreto, a 'strange building' containing the Black Madonna is said to have appeared suddenly, overnight, on 10 May 1291 – an event that the parish priest claimed to have been told of in the course of a dream.

The Black Madonna of Montserrat was supposedly discovered by shepherds in a cave in 880 AD, after they had been led to it by nocturnal celestial lights and angelic choirs. At Avioth, in north-east France, the Black Madonna is reputed suddenly to have materialised in a thorn bush. At Le Puy, she is said first to have appeared in a vision and to have commanded that a church be built on the site in her honour. The plan for the building is said to have been outlined by a fall of snow in midsummer; and its consecration, a century or so later, was allegedly attended by celestial lights and choirs.

HEAVENLY MILK

The Madonna, and the Black Madonna in particular, first assumed a crucial position in Christendom during the Middle Ages and the period of the Crusades. In large part ,this was due to the influence of Saint Bernard (1090-1153), the famous abbot of Clairvaux in France, who probably did more than any other individual to propagate the cult of the Virgin. Saint Bernard himself is said to have experienced his most dramatic religious illumination from the Black Madonna of Châtillon. While he was reciting the Ave Marias before her, she reportedly pressed her breast, whereupon three drops of milk fell into the monk's open mouth.

The 'Queen of Heaven' also became the official patroness of the Knights Templar and, later, of their German equivalent, the Teutonic Order. She figured widely on chivalric banners and standards, and knights took the field in her honour, their battle cry often consisting solely of her name. In a sense, she absorbed the whole of the Christian Trinity – Father, Son and Holy Ghost. Indeed, as 'Bride of God', in many respects the Virgin effectively displaced the Trinity.

In the text of the *Mass of the Immaculate Conception of the Virgin,* there is even the following statement: 'The Lord possessed me at the beginning of His ways. I existed before He formed any creature. I existed from all eternity, before the earth was created... '

While the Virgin was sometimes referred to as the 'Bride of God', she was also known as the 'Mother of God'. For some medieval Catholic writers, it was even the Virgin, not God, who created

// LET ME SAY WHY I THINK THIS PRESIDING IMAGE OF THE WORLD'S HOPE-IN-LOVE IS REPRESENTED AS BLACK... BECAUSE SHE IS THE SYMBOL AND GATEWAY TO EVERYTHING WE COULD KNOW IN THE APPARENT BLACKNESS BEYOND VISIBLE SIGHT. //

PETER REDGROVE, THE BLACK GODDESS AND THE SIXTH SENSE

The Black Madonna at Einsiedeln, Switzerland, below, *richly adorned as it is with gold and jewels, demonstrates the degree of veneration in which these unusual statues are held.*

the world. The whole of existence was believed to have depended upon her. According to one writer: 'At the command of Mary, all obey, even God.' She was frequently equated with the Holy Ghost – who was often symbolised, like the Virgin, by a dove. Indeed, the Holy Ghost is regarded as feminine in Hebrew and was also considered to be such by the early Christian church.

HOLY MEDIATOR

During the Middle Ages, then, Christianity – particularly in the popular mind – centred primarily on the Virgin. It became, in effect, a matriarchal rather than a patriarchal religion – a religion orientated more around the feminine principle than the masculine. God, the Father, ceased to dominate the popular mind as He had previously. Jesus, the Son, became increasingly feminine in character, with emphasis placed upon his meekness, gentleness and passivity. And the Virgin became the mediator between God and Man – the guardian of all western Europe in many respects.

The great Gothic cathedrals of this time also became her temples and palaces. Indeed, between 1170 and 1270, no less than 80 cathedrals and 500 churches to 'Our Lady' were erected in France alone. A significant number of these edifices were constructed on sites already hallowed by the presence not merely of a Madonna statue, but of a Black Madonna. While it cannot be proved definitely, it has been argued that all the major cathedrals to Our Lady were actually built on former Black Madonna sites.

Yet the Church of Rome, as we have seen, appears at times to have been rather embarrassed by the Black Madonna statues. Officially, it refused to distinguish them from the more conventional 'white' Madonnas. At the same time, however,

many of them were white-washed or, as in the case of the Black Madonna of Avioth, painted over in a flesh colour. Elaborate attempts were also made to rationalise the statues' blackness. Some of these rationalisations were plausible enough. The wood, in some cases, might well have been blackened by smoke or age. In some cases, the silver in which the statues were often swaddled might well have oxidised, thus darkening the wood. But the fact remains that most of the statues were carved originally from ebony – a black wood – or from black stone. In other words, it seems that they were intended to be black from the very beginning. This would also seem to be confirmed by the fact that Black Madonnas have been produced in relatively modern times and are almost certainly deliberately black – the Black Madonna installed at Orval, for example.

It has been suggested that the worship or devotion accorded the Black Madonnas was never strictly orthodox, nor truly in accord with established Catholic dogma. And indeed, many beliefs associated with Black Madonnas are not only non-Christian in both nature and origin – they are clearly pagan. Many of the Black Madonnas are associated with sexuality, procreation and fertility – hardly the traditional qualities attributed to the Virgin Mary. The Black Madonna of Montserrat is even honoured at festivals by a circular (orgiastic) ritual dance of unmistakably pagan derivation. Other Black Madonnas, like the one at Chartres, are identified as 'Queen of the Underworld'. Others still are explicitly associated with the moon, or with the planet Venus. Such associations do not seem to tally with the traditional image of Jesus' pure and immaculate virgin mother.

So it certainly seems that, if the Black Madonnas do represent the Virgin Mary, they must also, clearly, represent something else.

PERSPECTIVES

THE CULT OF THE VIRGIN MARY

Mary, Mother of God, plays a key role in the Roman Catholic Church. She is believed to possess miraculous powers and to have ascended into Heaven without having suffered bodily corruption. She is also believed to be a living person who intervenes directly in the affairs of Man. While these beliefs are specifically Christian, they are also thought by some to have originated in pagan beliefs stretching back 10,000 years before the birth of Christ. It is these beliefs that are generally considered to mark the beginnings of the cult of the Virgin Mary and the origins of the Black Madonnas.

Long before the appearance of male gods, primitive Man is supposed to have worshipped a female Creator. This Goddess, because she came before the male, was believed to have been a virgin. The cycle of birth was shrouded in mystery. Since sex did not always lead to birth, it was believed that birth could occur without sex – by swallowing a blade of grass,

In the depiction of the Madonna and Child, above, *the lilies in her hand symbolise purity.*

for example, or standing against the wind. The Goddess alone controlled the mysterious cycle of fertility, conception and birth.

Originally, the Virgin was not accorded any greater honours than other saints. But to survive the shocks suffered after the sacking of Rome in 410 AD, the early Church, it has been suggested, grafted on to Mary, mother of Christ, attributes hitherto accorded to the Goddess. Both were known as the 'Queen of Heaven', as 'Protectress' and 'Virgin Mother'. In place of the Christian concept of the all-male Trinity – Father, Son and Holy Ghost – the Church now emphasised the place of Mary, the female principle. This struck a chord in the popular imagination which had always held the female, in some sense, to be higher than the male. Mary fulfilled this role in a way that the Trinity never could.

Within the Eastern Church, too, the role of the Virgin Mary, as evidenced by her presence on icons, is particularly significant.

THE WITCH-HUNTS OF SALEM

THE VERY WORDS 'WITCH-HUNT' SUMMON UP A PICTURE OF MINDLESS, HYSTERICAL PERSECUTION OF THE INNOCENT. THIS WOULD CERTAINLY APTLY DESCRIBE THE UGLY EVENTS THAT TOOK PLACE IN THE AMERICAN TOWN OF SALEM

Salem's usually sedate courtroom assumes the riotous madness of Bedlam, below. In just 10 months, the God-fearing Puritan community had – merely on the accusations of some teenage girls who were experimenting with the occult – executed 20 people on charges of witchcraft.

Just after Christmas 1691, seven young girls of Salem Village, situated in Essex County, Massachusetts, USA, took up fortune-telling in order to while away the long winter months. They used an egg poured into a wine glass as a 'crystal ball' in an attempt to see whether they could.conjure up images of their future husbands. But instead, according to the Rev. John Hale of nearby Beverly: 'There came up a coffin, that is, a specter in likeness of a coffin.'

It was to be an apt omen. Only 10 months later, as a direct result of the girls' experiments, the little Puritan community lay devastated. Twenty people had been executed for witchcraft, while over 100 more lay in prison, their property confiscated, and the name of Salem had become a synonym for mindless and cruel persecution. As a Boston merchant, Thomas Brattle, wrote prophetically: 'I am afraid that ages will not wear off that reproach and those stains which these things will leave behind them upon our land.'

Compared with the great witch-hunts of Europe, those of Salem were hardly widespread. In the mid-17th century, for instance, an estimated 900 witches had been burned in the city of Bamburg alone, and as many as 5,000 in the province of Alsace; while in the English county of Essex – from which the Massachusetts district took its name – the 'Witchfinder General' Matthew Hopkins dispatched to the gallows at least twice as many victims as were to be executed at Salem.

But Salem's abiding horror lies in the fact that it was the last major instance of a sober, rational and industrious society tearing itself apart through a dreadful fear of the Devil. The details of how it did so exist in abundance – in voluminous court records, over 50 written 'confessions', ecclesiastical journals and contemporary letters. Yet despite two centuries of historical analysis, the reason why the reign of terror took place at Salem still remains largely conjectural.

'When these calamities first began,' wrote the Rev. Samuel Parris, 'which was in my own family, the affliction was several weeks before such hellish operations as witchcraft were suspected.'

Parris was minister of Salem Village and, like the majority of Massachusetts clergymen of the time, a Puritan. However, the New England Puritans had, by the 1690s, become a remarkably tolerant and well-balanced society. Ingersoll's Tavern in Salem Village was patronized by clergy and laity alike, people 'living in sin' were frowned upon but unmolested, and true poverty was almost non-existent. Intellectually, standards were high; Harvard University, on the outskirts of Boston, 15 miles (24 kilometres) to the south of Salem Village, was founded largely through the efforts of the Rev. Increase Mather, who was to play a prominent advisory part in the witchcraft trials; and Samuel Sewell, one of the Salem judges, was writing his tract *The Selling of Joseph,* the first anti-slavery pamphlet published in America, at the time.

Prosecutions for witchcraft – despite a widespread belief in the Devil and his works – were rare. Only half-a-dozen 'witches' had been hanged in the province during the entire 17th century, while a handful more were sentenced to the relatively mild punishments of whipping, fines or exile. In fact, almost every village had its 'wise' man or woman, to whom the residents went for healing potions and love charms. The Rev. Cotton Mather, Increase's son, who was to gain an unjustly infamous name during the Salem persecutions, took a tolerant and relatively scientific interest in witchcraft. A former medical student and fellow of the Royal Society, he even invited a number of 'possessed' persons into his own home, first searching for signs of organic illness before 'treating' them by means of prayer and fasting.

It was to prayer and fasting that the Rev. Parris turned when his nine-year-old daughter Elizabeth and 11-year-old niece Abigail Williams began to throw fits after experimenting with the glass and egg. Five other girls were also affected: 12-year-old

Ann Putnam and four older girls, Elizabeth Hubbard, Mary Walcott, Mary Warren and Mercy Lewis, whose ages ranged from 16 to 20. The Rev. Parris wisely removed his daughter and niece to the home of a friend in Salem Town, 5 miles (8 kilometres) away; the remaining five were to form the 'accusers'.

'Their motions in their fits are preternatural,' wrote the Rev. Deodat Lawson, 'both as to the manner, which is so strange as a well person could not screw their body into; and as to the violence... it is... much beyond the ordinary force of the same person when they are in their right mind.'

Later, the girls suffered hallucinations, seeing 'spectral' figures who beat, scratched and bit them – often leaving actual marks on their flesh – and struck them temporarily blind, deaf and dumb. They also suffered loss of appetite and had choking attacks. In fact, they all exhibited classic symptoms of what is now recognized as hysteria – in the clinical, rather than the colloquial, sense of the word. As one modern author, Chadwick Hansen, put it: 'With minor exceptions, the girls' behaviour belongs to the history of pathology rather than the history of fraud.' But practical psychiatry lay 200 years in the future. When the Rev. Parris finally took the girls to the local doctor, William Griggs, he announced: 'The Evil Hand is upon them'. In other words, he believed they were bewitched.

COUNTER-SPELL

Once that seemed to have been established, at least the lay people of Salem knew what to do. Mary Walcott's aunt, Mary Sibley, visited the Rev. Parris' Carib Indian slaves, John and Tituba, and asked them to bake a cake of meal mixed with the girls' urine – an ancient counter-spell against curses – which, on 25 February 1692, was fed to the Parris family dog. The 'spell' worked; the dog died, and the girls were able to name their tormentors – Tituba, the slave, and two local 'wise women', Sarah Good and Sarah Osburn.

When he heard about the cake, the Rev. Parris was appalled: like other contemporary clergymen, he believed that 'counter-spells' were as sinful as the original spells. Through the 'witch cake', he said: 'The Devil hath been raised among us, and his rage is vehement and terrible; and when he shall be silenced, the Lord only knows.'

Revelation of 'guilty names' had set the wheels of justice in motion, for on 29 February four 'yeomen of Salem Village' swore out warrants for the arrest of Tituba, Sarah Good and Sarah Osburn, and the following day they were brought before the community's two magistrates, John Hathorne and Jonathan Corwin. Hathorne, in particular, seems instantly to have adopted an inquisitorial, rather than magisterial, role, assuming the guilt of the parties before they were even asked to plead. 'Sarah Good,' he asked, 'what evil spirits have you familiarity with? Have you made no contract with the Devil? Why do you thus torment these poor children?' – and so on. In the case of Sarah Good, he may have felt justified, for her own husband, William, testified that he thought she was either 'a witch or would be one very quickly' because of her 'bad carriage to him'; and her four-year-old daughter Dorcas claimed that her mother kept black and yellow birds as familiars that 'hurt the children and afflicted persons'.

Contemporary records tell how, when the girls were asked to face Sarah Good and say whether she was one of their tormentors, they all immediately fell into fits and 'were dreadfully tortured and tormented for a short space of time'. When recovered, they said that Good's 'spectre' had come and tormented them, 'though her body remained at a considerable distance from them.'

This introduction of what became known as 'spectral evidence' was to be a cause of dissension between the clergy and the judiciary. Among its prominent opponents was Cotton Mather, who pointed out that: 'The odd effects produced upon the sufferers by the look or touch of the accused are things wherein the Devils may as much impose upon some harmless people as by the representation of their shapes.'

In other words, if the Devil had power to run loose in Salem, he also had, in the words of Hamlet, 'power to assume a pleasing shape'. Only

A 'bewitched' girl, above, falls in convulsions before a Salem court. No matter how wild her accusations, wherever she pointed her finger some wretch was arrested, accused of sorcery and imprisoned, fined or even hanged, as a model scene from the Salem Witch Museum, right, shows.

clear evidence of a 'pact' between an accused person and the Devil should be admitted, insisted Mather, otherwise 'innocent, aye virtuous' people were at risk. But the magistrates were, perhaps understandably, deeply impressed by the fact that the girls always flew into fits when faced with, or touched by, an 'accused' person.

In vain, Robert Pike, a magistrate from nearby Salisbury, pointed out that it would be the height of folly for a person pleading innocent to charges of witchcraft at the same time to perform those very acts of witchcraft in the courtroom by causing the girls to have fits. 'Self-interest,' he said, 'teaches everyone better.'

In the cases of the first three women, however, there was little need to convict them on 'spectral evidence'. Sarah Good, a vicious old woman according to her own husband's testimony, was known to mutter under her breath when passing people who

Salem is a thriving tourist attraction in Massachusetts. Visitors enjoy taking photographs of the witch house, above, and of Gallows Hill, left – which, in another location, might be an ideal picnic spot. In the summer, Salem is crowded with sightseers, but three centuries ago it was a place to be avoided.

had annoyed her – so surely she must be reciting curses? Sarah Osburn admitted that she had dreamed of 'a thing like an Indian, all black, which did prick her in the neck' – so, surely, this was the Devil 'marking her' for his own?

But the evidence of the slave Tituba was most sensational of all, and opened a new dimension of unease – it seemed that an organized coven was operating in the neighbourhood. She had, she said, met the Devil in the shape of a tall black man with white hair. Sometimes he had come in the shape of an animal. He had brought a book and made her place her mark in it, 'red like blood', thus binding her to him for six years. There had been nine marks altogether in the book, two of them made by Good and Osburn, and two made by 'witches from Boston'. Both Good and Osburn, she said, had familiars: cats, birds, and a 'thing with wings and two legs and a head like a woman'. Most disturbing of all, Osburn had 'a thing all over hairy, all the face hairy, and a long nose, and I don't know how to tell how the face looks.' It had two legs, she said, 'and goeth upright like a man, and last night it stood in Mr Parris' hall.'

The three women were committed to jail. Osburn died there on 10 May, and the slave Tituba was left there until she was sold to pay her jailer's fees – the Rev. Parris being too shocked, no doubt, by the revelations of what had gone on in his house to pay them. Sarah Good awaited sentence.

Meanwhile, Friday, 11 March was appointed as a day of fasting and prayer, during which the ministers of Essex County would meet for a consultation. But instead of agreement, another seed of dissension was sown when the girls did just what Cotton Mather feared: they accused a respectable church member, Martha Corey, of witchcraft.

Martha Corey had been sceptical from the first of the 'witchcraft' charges, even refusing to allow her husband to visit the magistrate's examinations. When she expressed her scepticism in court – 'we must not believe all that these distracted children say' – she annoyed Judge Hathorne. But much more damning, when she bit her lip in concentration, the children complained of being 'bitten' in the same place, the marks showing clearly.

Again the clergy, in the person of the Rev. Deodat Lawson, cautioned the magistrates against

Martha Corey, a highly respectable member of the community, is depicted below, being asked to sign a confession that she is a witch. This was what the Rev. Cotton Mather had feared – that the witch-hunt was a contagion from which no one, no matter what his or her previous reputation, was safe. But the most spectacular terror was engendered by the 'evidence' of the slave Tituba, bottom, who told of a local coven, familiars and all. There was no real evidence to support this allegation – but in the prevailing atmosphere, none was needed.

precipitous action. In church, Lawson preached that 'rash censuring of others, without sufficient grounds... is indeed to be like the Devil, who... is a false accuser.'

But the damage had been done. On the very day of Lawson's sermon, one of the most benevolent members of the community, a regular church-goer, Rebecca Nurse, was accused. Even Judge Hathorne was uncertain at this turn of events, as his questioning shows; and he expressed his doubts and prayed that God might 'clear you if you be innocent'. Nevertheless, precedents had been established, and the community was beginning to think the testimony of the children infallible.

One sane – if rather brutal – voice spoke out. A farmer named John Proctor, who employed one of the afflicted girls, Mary Warren, as a servant, rode into the village to 'fetch home his jade', as he put it. Dragging her off, he said: 'If they were let alone, we should all be devils and witches quickly. They should be had to the whipping post.' It was his intention, he said, to 'keep her close to the wheel and thrash her'. Curiously, just as a slap in the face

" WHEN A VICTIM WAS BEWITCHED, THERE WERE WAYS OF IDENTIFYING THE WITCH AND BREAKING THE SPELL, MOST DRASTICALLY BY LYNCHING HER OR BY DEMANDING THAT THE AUTHORITIES TRY HER AND EXECUTE HER, FOR HER DEATH WOULD AUTOMATICALLY DISSOLVE HER MAGIC. "

RICHARD CAVENDISH,

A HISTORY OF MAGIC

stops hysterical laughter, Proctor's whipping may have done Mary Warren some good, for she was the only one of the girls who completely recovered her sanity.

Next Dorcas Good, Sarah Good's four-year-old daughter, volunteered that she herself had a little snake as a 'familiar', which sucked at a spot on her hand. The examiners noticed such a spot 'about the bigness of a flea bite'. Incredibly, they accepted the 'confession' of the toddler without question. The Rev. Parris further confused matters by preaching a sermon to the effect that, as Judas had betrayed Christ, so a devout church member – Rebecca Nurse – might well be the servant of Satan in disguise. When Rebecca's sister, Sarah Cloyse, heard this, she got up and left the church, slamming the door behind her. It was enough: next day, the girls pointed the finger at her – and she, too, was accused on 4 April, along with Elizabeth Proctor, wife of the farmer who had saved Mary Warren.

LAW, ORDER – AND LUNACY

At this point, four other magistrates were appointed to sit with Corwin and Hathorne, including Thomas Danforth, deputy governor of the colony; but it was Hathorne, the bit firmly between his teeth, who continued to be the driving force. John Proctor joined his wife in the dock, closely followed by his servant Mary Warren. 'Cured' by the whipping she had received, she in turn was accused by her former fellow sufferers.

On 19 April, Giles Corey, husband of Martha, Corey, was dragged before the court along with two new suspects, a young girl named Abigail Hobbes and a woman called Bridget Bishop who had a long-standing reputation as a witch. Abigail Hobbes was a prankster who loved shocking her elders. Once, she had mocked the sacrament of baptism by pouring water over her mother's head, and on another occasion had told a friend that she had 'sold herself body and soul to the Old Boy' – presumably the Devil.

Bridget Bishop had been accused of witchcraft 10 years previously, but had been released when the Rev. Hale defended her. Nevertheless, it is likely that she was one of the three or four 'real' witches turned up by the Salem enquiry. Witch dolls stuck with pins were found in her house; and certainly, many people willingly testified to her malice and her open avowal of supernatural powers.

Another 'real' witch was Candy, a black slave from Barbados, who gave a demonstration of her 'powers' in court by tying knots in rags. These were first burned and then placed under water, and the afflicted girls suffered spectacularly: one was 'presently burned on the hand', while two were 'choked and strived for breath as if underwater'.

Cotton Mather was later to point out that, by allowing these experiments to take place, the magistrates themselves were actively condoning witchcraft, but by this time any means of combating the 'evil' seemed permissible, so deep did it run. For it was one thing to accuse the likes of Bridget Bishop, Candy, Dorcas Hoar, the Beverly 'wise woman', and 'Mammy' Redd, 'town witch' of Marblehead, but quite another to find a former minister of Salem Village in the dock, as we shall see in a forthcoming feature.

BY THE TIME THE WITCH-HUNT OF SALEM HAD RUN ITS COURSE, WHOLE FAMILIES HAD BEEN RUINED AND THE VERY NAME OF THE VILLAGE HAD BECOME SYNONYMOUS WITH MINDLESS PERSECUTION. BUT WERE ALL OF THE ACCUSED TOTALLY INNOCENT?

On 20 April 1692, 12-year-old Ann Putnam saw the apparition of a Puritan minister who had half strangled her. Ann, one of the 'bewitched' girls of Salem Village, Massachusetts, USA, asked her ghostly tormentor who he was. Obligingly, he told her: he was the Rev. George Burroughs, who had been minister at the village between 1680 and 1682 – when Ann was two years old.

'She was greviously affrighted,' according to evidence presented to the witchcraft court, 'and cried out: "Oh dreadful, dreadful. Here is a minister come. What, are ministers witches too?"'

In this case, the court decided that George Burroughs was, indeed, a witch. He was recalled from the village in Maine where he held his present living, and brought back to Salem to answer the charges against him. To Judge John Hathorne, Burroughs' position in the community made him an obvious leader of the oddly assorted collection of 'witches' already arrested. Burroughs, a short, stocky man, had been suspected by popular gossip of doing away with both his wives while minister at Salem. Now Ann Putnam confirmed the rumours: she had seen the wraiths of the two women, she said, and they had told her that they had been victims of their husband's witchcraft.

SALEM'S GRIM LEGACY

When strange things happened at Salem, such as the wolf attack, **above, *it was frequently blamed on witchcraft. The notorious history of this Massachusetts village is commemorated by the sign,*** **left.**

The engraving, left, shows an accusing finger being pointed at two condemned 'witches' during the Salem trials.

The illustration below shows witches on a flight to an unholy sabbat. Was it mere fantasy, or were there really witches at Salem?

England judges – who, acting on the written advice of Cotton Mather, tended towards leniency at first. Mather stressed that 'it is better that ten witches go free than that one innocent person be convicted'; but, on 10 June, the court claimed its first victim, Bridget Bishop.

On 19 July, the malicious Sarah Good, the innocent Rebecca Nurse, and three other women followed Bridget Bishop to the gallows. As she climbed the gallows steps, Sarah Good made a prediction that some were to think, in retrospect, proved her guilt. When the Rev. Nicholas Noyes asked her to repent of her witchcraft, she cried out: 'You are a liar. I am no more a witch than you are a wizard, and if you take away my life, God will give you blood to drink.' A quarter of a century later, Noyes suffered a massive lung haemorrhage and choked on his own blood. Judge Hathorne's great-great-grandson, Nathaniel Hawthorne, used the incident in his novel *The House of Seven Gables*.

On 19 August, five more people, including the Rev. George Burroughs and the whip-wielding farmer John Proctor, were hanged on Gallows Hill. Burroughs made a good impression on the crowd by reciting the Lord's Prayer perfectly – something no witch was supposed to be able to do. But Cotton Mather addressed the spectators from horseback,

Goodman Ruck, Burroughs' former brother-in-law, told the court that, on one occasion, when he and his sister had been out picking strawberries with Burroughs, the minister had left them for a while and had rejoined them further along the road, when he was able to repeat the conversation they had held in his absence. When they expressed surprise, Burroughs had told them: 'My God makes known your thoughts unto me' – by which, Ruck explained, he meant the Devil.

EAVESDROPPER

Unfortunately for Burroughs, he was apparently in the habit of hiding, listening to conversations, and then reporting them verbatim to his astonished listeners – not a trick liable to endear him to the hysterical inhabitants of Salem.

Despite his small stature, his broad shoulders gave Burroughs enormous strength, which he had used to impress the community. There is also evidence to suggest that he used tricks to enhance his strong-arm reputation, appearing to lift a 7-foot (2-metre) musket simply by inserting his forefinger in the barrel, for instance, and picking up a barrel of molasses between finger and thumb. The magistrates, however, took these tales as evidence of supernatural power; and when it was 'revealed' that Burroughs had made his wives sign oaths of secrecy about his exploits, he was finished.

Although some of those who had confessed so far – Tituba, for instance, and Dorcas Good – were spared, for others the enquiry had become a hanging matter. On 27 May, Governor William Phips, who – assisted by the Rev. Increase Mather – had been negotiating a new charter for Massachusetts, turned away from more pressing business to establish a special Court of Oyer and Terminer. These courts, abolished in 1972, were set up especially by Royal Commission to enquire into serious criminal matters. Phips appointed the cream of New

The House of Seven Gables in Salem, top, was the setting for Nathaniel Hawthorne's novel of the same name. Hawthorne was a direct descendant of Judge Hathorne, a central character in the witch-hunt.

Lori Cabot, top right, became a lecturer in witchcraft at the modern Salem State College.

The Rev. George Burroughs, above, was hanged as a witch at Salem. His unorthodox habits and interest in diabolism made his execution certain.

maintaining that the Devil could appear as 'an angel of light'. This move, more than his repeated appeals for leniency and common sense, blackened Mather's name for posterity. But he had recommended that Proctor's wife, Elizabeth, be spared. She had been condemned to death with him, but was allowed to 'plead her belly' – she was pregnant – and was later released.

PRESSING TORTURE

In September came one of the bravest stands against the increasing madness of the court. Giles Corey, husband of Martha Corey, refused to recognize the impartiality of his judges, and was thus subjected to *peine forte et dure* – pressing with heavy weights – to make him answer the charges. He died after two days of this torture on 19 September, still silent. 'His tongue being pressed out of his mouth,' recorded one contemporary, 'the sheriff with his cane forced it in again when he was dying.'

A rather less dramatic stand had been taken by Captain John Alden of Boston, who had been accused by the demented girls while on a visit to Salem. He stood in court, 'a bold fellow with his hat on before the judges', and it was said that he 'sells powder and shot to the Indians and the French, and lies with the Indian squaws and has Indian papooses'. When one of the magistrates, Bartholomew Gedney, remarked how the witnesses fell down when Alden looked on them, Alden asked 'what reason there could be given why Alden's looking upon him did not strike him down as well, but no reason was given...'

Alden later escaped from jail and made his way to New York, returning when the witch-hunt was over. But eight more people, including Martha Corey and the 'wise woman', Mammy Redd, were executed on 22 September. By now, an air of black farce was creeping in; one man, for instance, was

accused of 'firing a mare's fart' by sticking a lighted tobacco pipe up its anus in order to relieve a belly ache. And when the girls were taken to Andover – a small town quieter, if anything, than even Salem Village had been previously – they claimed that 'there were forty men in it that could raise the Devil as well as any astrologer... '

In fact, over 50 people were 'complained of' in Andover; and when the local magistrate Dudley Bradstreet had signed 'thirty or forty warrants', he came to his senses and refused to grant more. Predictably, he and his wife were immediately accused, and fled to New Hampshire. Bradstreet's brother, John, was also forced to flee; his dog was therefore executed instead.

DROPPED CHARGES

Cotton Mather's prediction that 'worthy people' would be caught up in the general panic was gradually coming true. One Boston merchant threatened to sue his accusers to the tune of £1,000, upon which the charges were promptly dropped. Other people 'accused' but not proceeded against included Judge Nathaniel Saltonstall, who had resigned from the court in protest at its inhumanity, Phillip English, a relative of Judge Hathorne, and the mother-in-law of Judge Corwin – a lady named Mrs Margaret Thatcher.

Increase and Cotton Mather renewed their protest at the admission of 'spectral evidence'; and by late summer, 'excepting Mr Hales, Mr Noyse, and Mr Parris, the Reverend Elders throughout the country [were] very much dissatisfied.' On 29 October, the clergy, led by Increase Mather, presented a bill before the General Court of Massachusetts in Boston, calling for the dismissal of the Court of Oyer and Terminer that had been set up. The bill also called for a 'fast day' that they 'might be led in the right way towards the witchcrafts'. The witch-hunt, by now, was all but over.

Then began the recriminations and the allocation of blame. After a long argument, the Rev. Parris was dismissed from the Salem Village living in 1697, on the grounds that he had been 'the beginner and procurer' of the trouble by publicizing the girls' 'possession' in the first place.

The excommunications of several church members, including Martha Corey and Rebecca Nurse, were posthumously lifted; while survivors such as Elizabeth Proctor who, because of their sentences, had been unable to inherit the property of their executed relatives, were compensated by the court. But the heartbreak suffered by many in the community was not to be lifted so easily. One petition, sent to the General Court set up in 1710 to investigate, speaks for many:

'My wife... was in prison about four months and then executed. A sucking child died in prison before the mother's execution. A child of four or five... was in prison seven or eight months, and being chained in the dungeon was so hardly used and terrified that she hath ever since been very chargeable, having little or no reason to govern herself. And I leave it unto the honorable Court to judge what damage I have sustained by such a destruction of my poor family... '

A CRYING SHAME

Seven women, including Bridget Bishop and Mammy Redd, never did receive a reversal of their attainders – a pardon. The nearest their descendants got was a statement given in a resolution by the General Court of Massachusetts as late as 1957, to the effect that:

'Whereas... certain descendants... are still distressed by the record of said proceedings [the witchcraft trials]... the General Court of Massachusetts declares its belief that such proceedings... were and are shocking... and as all the laws under which said proceedings, even if then legally conducted, have been long since abandoned and superseded by our more civilized laws, no disgrace or cause for distress attached to the said descendants... '

In the 1950s, Senator Joe McCarthy, above, unleashed an anti-Communist hysteria reminiscent of that of the Salem witch-hunt. Among his many victims was Charlie Chaplin, right, whose career suffered a severe setback because of McCarthy's campaign, although he was innocent. Another victim was writer Arthur Miller, whose play The Crucible, a scene from which is seen below, was based on the Salem trials. It contains thinly veiled references to McCarthy.

There were undoubtedly strange things going on at Salem. And the 'seance' that first set the girls off into pathological hysteria has exact parallels in well-attested modern cases.

The evidence of Tituba, the Carib Indian slave, when taken as a whole, seems to indicate that she had at least some of the characteristics of an excellent medium.

Rev. George Burroughs, trickery apart, did have a deep knowledge of diabolism, and behaved very oddly for a Puritan minister. He even admitted that he had not taken communion for years, and only the eldest of his children had been baptized. And there can be little doubt about the efficacy of at least some of the spells cast by the many 'village wise women' who had been called before the Salem courts. Anthropologists have shown repeatedly that witchcraft works in societies that believe in it.

But the blind and mindless horror brought down by otherwise benevolent men on their own people, swiftly followed by apparently sincere shame and repentance for what they had done, is of a deeper order entirely. When the anti-Communist 'witch-hunts' of the McCarthyite 1950s were seen in retrospect to compare so closely with the events in Salem Village, it seemed that Man's own devilish power to wreak havoc among the virtuous had not diminished with the passing of time.

43

SECRETS OF THE SEX CULTS

IS THE CULT OF TANTRA SIMPLY AN EXCUSE FOR SEXUAL EXCESSES, AS CLAIMED BY ITS CRITICS? OR ARE ITS RITUALS INDEED THE KEY TO ULTIMATE SPIRITUAL SALVATION?

The entire universe is in perfect equilibrium, its two primary polarities precisely balanced – like a god and goddess locked together in divine and intimate union. The highest spiritual goal, therefore, is for humanity to attain resonance with that unsurpassable state through sexual rituals. So say the followers of Tantra, a cult that originated in

Shiva, the major male god of Tantra, is seen above, dancing upon a dwarf demon and encircled by symbols of creation, destruction and rebirth. Tantrism has a whole pantheon of deities and a complex ideology of spiritual fulfilment.

the ancient East and that has enjoyed popularity among Western occultists and mystics since at least the end of the 19th century. It continues to flourish – largely in secret – today.

To the outsider, its rites may seem nothing more than an indulgence in promiscuous and apparently obscene sex. Even worse, perhaps, the rituals seem to smack of utter depravity and black magic. But in its purest sense, Tantrism is nothing of the kind. Tantra, from which the cult's name is derived, is a Sanskrit word meaning 'warp'. It signifies a body of written teaching – the warp – through which are threaded the supplementary oral and physical training and preparation – the weft – needed for the attainment of personal and direct experience of God, the gods, the Universal Essence, the Ultimate – however the seeker after wisdom and salvation chooses to envisage this awesome goal.

In fact, the sexually explicit, erotic and, to some, disgusting aspects of Tantric rites take up only a small percentage of the entire written texts. Yet it is probably true to say that these practices, and the powers they are supposed to confer, are the main factor in the cult's appeal to Westerners.

Tantrism has almost always been practised in secret. And, in spite of the increased sexual freedom and permissiveness of the late 20th century, it is still a secret cult. Although the oldest texts date back only to around the end of the 10th century, it is said that there were many more ancient ones, which were destroyed by successive invaders of the Indus Valley and by orthodox Hindus who tried to stamp out Tantra. Libraries of Tantric scripts were burned, the cult's monasteries were razed, and priests were put to death. Not surprisingly, surviving teachers and followers went into hiding. Tantra, however, has much to offer besides the sexual practices that offended the persecutors and that appal modern critics.

In Tantric philosophy, the two major gods, who personify the balanced polarities of the cosmos, are

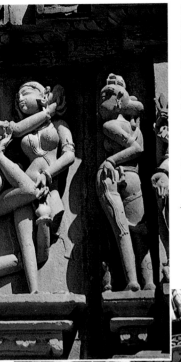

Shiva and his consort Shakti. But it is the female, Shakti, who is regarded as the superior of the two because she is seen as the primal, creative, active force – the Mother Goddess, Great Mother or Great Goddess. The Tantrics have no caste system, consider women completely equal to men and, in many rites, envisage the female partner as the physical vehicle of the goddess Shakti herself.

OCCULT PHILOSOPHY

The range of subjects that Tantrism treats is so broad that it covers almost all areas of occult philosophy including the creation and ultimate destruction of the world; an entire pantheon of deities; yoga and meditation; astral travel and heightened consciousness; prolonged longevity – and, of course, the sexual rites by which, it is believed, many powers and profound insights may be obtained. Indeed, more than one commentator has noted

THE SUCCESSFUL TANTRIC IS, IN FACT, A PART OF – AND ABLE TO MANIPULATE AT WILL – ANY SEGMENT OF THE COSMOS. IT IS A CASE OF SALVATION THROUGH SEX.

Shakti-yoga is the key to the real alchemical process indicated, and its exercises are based on the concept of the chakras, which might be defined as centres. Another name used almost synonymously with chakras is *padmas,* meaning 'lotuses'. Chakras are said to be located inside the body, but are not envisaged as physical organs. Rather, they are subtle physical centres of energy, located at each plexus (nerve centre) of the body.

There are seven major chakras in the human body, we are told. The lowest of these is called the *muladharà,* which is said to lie near the base of the spine. It is here that the feminine, active principle, the goddess Shakti herself, is believed to lie dormant. She is symbolised as a sleeping serpent, known as the *kundalini* – from *kundala* meaning 'coiled' – and she waits to be awakened and eventually conjoined with her counterpart Shiva, who is the male, passive principle.

Shiva, meanwhile, supposedly inhabits the *sahasrara* chakra – the 'thousand-petalled lotus' – that is to be found in the crown of the head. The way to bring these deities together, say the Tantrics, is to awaken Shakti and then cause her to move gradually up through the five intervening chakras of the body. These are the *svadhisthana,* above the genital region; the *manipura,* near the navel; the *anahata,* in the heart area; the *akasa,* in the throat; and the *ajna,* somewhere in the region of the pineal gland. The *ajna* is the so-called 'third

Despite such open display in art as the erotic sculptures on the Khajuraho temple in India, top and above, the Tantrics have nearly always practised their sexual rites in secret to escape persecution.

that the medieval grimoires and rituals of Western magic and sorcery seem to have been borrowed from eastern Tantrism and dressed it up in western trappings.

Long and difficult periods of preparation and training are essential for any form of attainment in the Tantric system. There are complex breathing exercises, gestures and postures, designed to lead to control of body temperature, pulse rate and other automatic physical functions. Intense and profound mental exercises are also performed, calculated to give total control to the will.

Successful adepts should ultimately be raised mentally, bodily and spiritually to attune their highest, inner essence to the Universal Spirit. This is often a religious goal, but there are many who would insist that Tantra is not a true religion.

The texts that describe the necessary techniques of Tantra are couched in highly allegorical and abstruse symbolism, designed to veil inner meaning. The sections dealing with spiritual alchemy, for example, at first sight appear to be describing nothing more than the physical effort of attempting to transmute base metals into gold. But they are actually intended to be applied internally.

The 19th-century drawing, right, shows the seven chakras (centres of energy). The lowest chakra is at the base of the spine, and here lies the kundalini, a snake symbolic of the goddess Shakti. Tantrics seek to awaken her and make her move up the body to the god Shiva, the highest chakra in the crown of the head. When this 'divine union' takes place, the Tantric has achieved his final goal, which takes years of rigorous training.

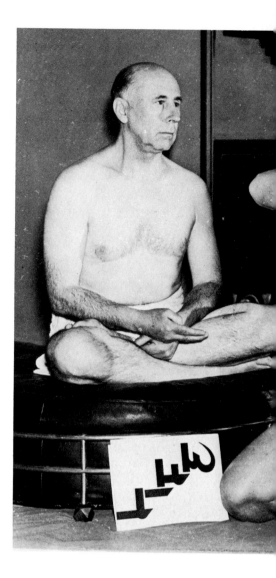

eye', beloved of eastern and western mystics alike as an organ of occult vision.

When the *kundalini* has reached the seventh chakra, Shakti and Shiva are united. The successful adept is then perfectly attuned to the Universe itself. This puts the enlightened one in a superior position to the rest of 'unawakened' mankind, leading as it does to the highest order of wisdom and power. The successful Tantric is, in fact, a part of – and able to manipulate at will – any segment or entity of the entire cosmos. It is, so it would appear, a case of salvation through sex.

But there are many pitfalls in this long, complex and arduous process of Tantric enlightenment and, if not undertaken properly with the aid of a knowledgeable master, dangers are very real. It is even said that if the *kundalini* force, which is likened to a kind of occult fire, gets out of control, madness or death can result.

The Tibetan bronze, above, is of the god Hevajra with his goddess Shakti. According to Tantric belief, such divine union keeps the Universe in perfect balance. The cult's sexual rituals aim to bring the cultists into resonance with this divine equilibrium.

▟▟ IF NOT UNDERTAKEN PROPERLY

WITH THE AID OF A KNOWLEDGEABLE

MASTER, DANGERS ARE VERY REAL.

IT IS EVEN SAID ... MADNESS AND

DEATH CAN RESULT. *▟▟*

Another of the dangers along the way is that aspirants could be diverted by mundane desires, born of their weaknesses and fanned by some of their achievements. The desire for wealth, longevity, or power over others, for instance, may seduce them away from the ultimate goal of divine union. And the sexual rites themselves, if not undertaken in the spirit of discipline that is intended, can obsess the practitioner to the point of bodily and mental collapse.

These rites – so often the target of the severest external criticism – involve nudity, group sex, incest and adultery. But although Tantrism has been described as a cult of ecstasy, it is not merely physical, sensual ecstasy that is paramount. Tantric rituals are deliberately designed to make the selection of a partner arbitrary. There is no emphasis on youth, beauty or mutual attraction.

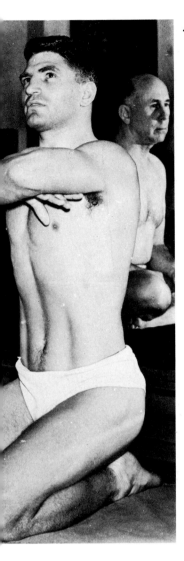

Lou Nova, above right, a boxing champion, is seen preparing for a major fight by taking muscle control instructions from Oom the Omnipotent, founder of an American cult with roots in Tantrism. Oom had a wealthy patron who established a permanent home for the cult in Nyack, New York.

The 17th -century Tibetan cloth painting, right, is of the Tantric Buddhas, including the Knowledge Holder, the Peaceful Buddhas, the Wrathful Buddhas and those presiding over the realms of reincarnation.

❝ ALTHOUGH TANTRISM HAS BEEN DESCRIBED AS A CULT OF ECSTASY, IT IS NOT MERELY PHYSICAL, SENSUAL ECSTASY THAT IS PARAMOUNT. TANTRIC RITUALS ARE DELIBERATELY DESIGNED TO MAKE THE SELECTION OF A PARTNER ARBITRARY. ❞

At higher levels of attainment, there are even claims of sexual intercourse with goddesses, elementals and female demons. One testimony to this has come from Stephen Jenkins, an English history teacher who was initiated into Tantric sexual ritual in Mongolia. In his book *The Undiscovered Country*, Jenkins explains that there are two stages in advanced Tantrism; one in which the female partner is an ordinary human being, and another in which she is 'a being of another order altogether'. The latter, he says, can take the form either of a 'skywalker' – spirits said to haunt western India and Ladak – or even of the Great Goddess Shakti herself. 'At the highest level of this particular method, the experience is indistinguishable from normal human intercourse at its intensest and most refined. I do not pretend to know how this works: I can only testify that it does,' he has said.

ELEMENTAL INTERCOURSE

It should be noted here that there are two different schools of Tantric sexual rites, known as the Right-Hand and Left-Hand Paths. It is believed that many of the cults that flourish secretly in the West today adhere to the Left-Hand Path. In Tantrism, this simply means that, in rites involving actual physical sex, the prospective female partners sit on the left-hand side of the male practitioners as the rite begins. In the Right-Hand Path, the sexual rites that take place are purely symbolic.

Francis King, a historian of ritual magic, wrote in *Sexuality, Magic and Perversion* that Edward Sellon (1818-1886) introduced Tantrism to Britain, although a few English and French academics had shown an interest in Hindu sex religion in the 18th century. Sellon – soldier, fencing master and pornographer – became acquainted with Tantric sexual rites in India, and his *Annotations on the Sacred Writings of the Hindus* appeared in 1865.

In the United States, possibly the first person to study and practise a form of sexual magic with some Tantric links was Paschal Beverley Randolph (1825-1871). He established various secret groups, one of which is believed to survive in France today. Like some Bengali practitioners of Tantra, Randolph used hallucinogenic drugs in his rites to attain heightened states of consciousness.

Another cult with distinctly Tantric overtones emerged in New York around 1919 under the name of the Brae Burn Club. It was headed by Pierre Bernard, who styled himself 'Oom the Omnipotent', and his wife, 'Mademoiselle de Vries', a vaudeville dancer whom he had taught the art of oriental danc-

ing and the basics of Tantrism. Mlle de Vries also promoted a so-called 'health system of Tantrism', attracting a succession of society people. Among these was a member of the Vanderbilt family, one of the wealthiest in the country. It was she who arranged for the Bernards to buy a mansion and estate at Nyack, New York, as a permanent home for the cult.

SECRET ORDER

The inner sanctum of this club was the 'Secret Order of Tantrics', whose members came to regard Bernard as a kind of man-god. Bernard and his wife aimed 'to teach men and women to love, and make women feel like queens' – a clear echo of the Tantric belief in the superiority of Shakti. One Tantric aphorism actually says: 'Shiva without Shakti is a corpse'.

Other occult groups had already adopted some of the sex magic associated with Tantra. During the late 19th century, for, instance, Karl Kellner, a wealthy German industrialist, had established an occult order based upon the sex magic he claimed he had learned while travelling in the East. This group developed into the Ordo Templi Orientis (OTO), branches of which spread throughout Europe and parts of Scandinavia. Occultist Aleister Crowley became the leader of the British OTO in 1922, but moved away from Tantric ideas and introduced elements such as 'magical masturbation' and homosexuality, adding degrees of adeptness of his own invention. He also used sex magic for temporal gain, which is not commensurate with traditional Tantric teaching. However, branches of the OTO continued to be established, and many still exist today, in the USA as well as Europe – evidence that western links with Tantric sexual ritual have survived into the late 20th century.

THE POWER OF WITCHCRAFT

PEOPLE FEAR WITCHCRAFT BECAUSE THEY BELIEVE THAT IT HAS A SUPERNATURAL CAPACITY TO HARM THEM. BUT DOES IT REALLY HAVE SUCH MAGICAL POWERS? AND HOW DID THE PRACTICE OF WITCHCRAFT FIRST ARISE?

Under the laws of Hammurabi, right, king of ancient Babylonia from around 1792 BC to 1750 BC, anyone accused of witchcraft was to be thrown into 'the holy river'. Persecution of witches, both by ducking and by burning, was common in Europe, too, from the medieval period onwards. A witch is 'swum' in the 16th-century engraving, below right, and another is burnt in a German illustration of 1555, far right. In the reign of Aethelstan of England, below, however, the punishment for witchcraft laid down in AD 924 was no more than a mere 120 days of imprisonment.

On 9 March 1967, an odd advertisement appeared in the Personal columns of *The Times*: 'A witch of full powers is urgently sought to lift a 73-year-old curse and help restore the family fortunes of an afflicted nobleman. Employment genuinely offered.'

Some days later, it was revealed that the advertiser was the bankrupt 74-year-old Duke of Leinster, head of one of Britain's oldest families. Over 170 people offered assistance. Whether or not witchcraft helped, the destitute duke was able eventually to pay off his debts, and was welcomed back into society before his death in the 1970s.

Some of the 'witches' who came to the ageing aristocrat's aid were followers of Gerald Gardner who invented much of modern witchcraft; others were members of 'independent' covens, and some were lone operators: all of them believed – or apparently believed – that they were inheritors of a craft that had passed from master to apprentice through the ages. But can any of their claims to magical powers be historically substantiated?

To begin with, there appears to have been no time or place on Earth where witchcraft and magic have not been practised. Man's attempt to control and come to terms with exterior natural phenomena through ritual and ceremony is an essential part of his way of thinking and behaving. Indeed, the evidence of primitive sculpture and cave painting suggests the eternal preoccupation of Man with magic and its effect on fertility, rainmaking, success in hunting, warding off sickness and evil influences; and 'modern' witches, students of Gardner, would claim these are their concerns, too.

By the time of the earliest written texts on magic, the Akkadean-Chaldean inscriptions of Nineveh dating from the second millennium BC, the practice of black and white magic had already developed into what E. M. Butler, in *Ritual Magic*, termed 'an extremely elaborate and well-developed demonology'. The practices described are almost identical to those associated with European witches in the Middle Ages. One inscription reads:

'He who has fashioned images corresponding to my whole appearance has bewitched my whole appearance; he has seized the magic draught prepared for me and has soiled my garments; he has torn my garments and has mingled his magic herb with the dust of my feet. May the fire-God, the hero, turn their magic to naught.'

The persecution of witches followed a familiar pattern, too. Hammurabi of Nineveh, in a legal code dating from the 17th century BC, laid down that:

'If a man has laid a charge of witchcraft on another man and has not justified it, he upon whom the witchcraft charge is laid shall go to the holy river, and if the holy river overcome him, he who accused him shall take to himself his house.'

The rules are rather different from 17th-century East Anglian witch-floating, but the instinct is very much the same.

The Bible even describes several encounters with witches, notably that between Saul and the witch of Endor. It also condemns them in texts that were used by medieval inquisitors to justify their own orgies of torture and burning. And wrongly, too, as it happens, since as early as 1584, Reginald Scot, in *Discovery of Witchcraft*, had pointed out that the most famous anti-witch text of all, 'Thou shalt not suffer a witch to live,' properly translates as 'Thou shalt not suffer poisoners to live.'

However, although *The Bible* speaks of individual practitioners of witchcraft, there is no evidence whatsoever to suggest that it was an organised religion of the kind claimed by Gerald Gardner and his followers.

MASS NECROMANCY

Many of the writers of ancient Greece also mention witchcraft as a practical reality, with necromancy – the raising of the dead – as one of its principal aims. Aeschylus, in his play *The Persians*, for example, describes the raising of Darius, while Homer in the ninth book of *The Odyssey* tells of a mass raising in gory detail.

The Romans Tacitus, Virgil, Horace, Tibullus, Livy and Pliny all describe witches as commonplace, and there is no doubt that witchcraft spread throughout the Roman Empire. After the break-up of the Empire in Britain, however, there are few literary mentions of witches, except as mild offenders against the law.

In the Saxon period, an edict was issued against those who 'practise any heathenship or in any way love witchcraft'. The penalty for such a crime was 10 half-marks: 'half to Christ, half to the King'. Under Aethelstan in AD 924, even when witchcraft had apparently been responsible for death, the punishment was only 120 days of imprisonment. This was rather more lenient than the law issued by the pious King Edgar, in AD 959, who ordained death for anyone disobeying his edict that on Christian

" THINK OF THE POWER WIELDED BY SATAN'S CHOSEN BRIDE! SHE CAN HEAL, PROPHESY, PREDICT, CONJURE UP THE SPIRITS OF THE DEAD, CAN SPELL-BIND YOU, CAN TURN YOU INTO A HARE OR A WOLF... AND MOST FATAL OF ALL, CAST A LOVE CHARM OVER YOU. "

JULES MICHELET,
SATANISM AND WITCHCRAFT

A witch-doctor, left, is seen offering cures at a market in Bali. Throughout Indonesia, witchcraft is accepted as a normal part of everyday life. In Europe, by contrast, witchcraft is generally regarded with suspicion, and the vogue that it enjoyed during the 1960s and 1970s was seen by many as threatening.

A detail from a 15th-century manuscript, below, shows members of the Manichee sect engaging in heretical practices. Primitive witchcraft was often confused with heresies such as Manicheism, and both were brutally dealt with by the Roman Catholic Church.

On the tablet, bottom, is inscribed 'May he who carried off Sylvia from me become as liquid as water. [May] he who obscenely devours her become dumb'.

feast days 'well worshippings, and necromancies and divinations and heathen songs and devil's games be abstained from.'

Undoubtedly, during this period there were still lingering traces of primitive 'heathenism' – the real 'Old Religion' of the pre-Christian era – throughout Britain. Many people clung determinedly to their old gods for several centuries after missionaries, such as Aidan and Columba, had begun preaching the Gospel. But those who continued to worship in the old ways were not by definition practitioners of witchcraft. In late Saxon and Norman times, there were indeed witches, but they tended to operate alone. William the Conqueror, for instance, called one in 'to disconcert by her magic all the warlike devices of the Saxons' at the siege of Ely in 1071. She was placed on a wooden siege tower that was promptly burned down by the defenders led by Hereward the Wake.

It was not until almost 100 years later, with the founding of the Inquisition in 1163 by the Council of Tours, that the Church began to confuse primitive witchcraft with the beliefs of such heretical sects as the Cathars and the Manichees. This misplaced notion gave rise to the ideas of Satanism and group Devil-worship by 'covynes' – Old French for 'coming together' or 'conspiracy' and from which the word 'coven' is derived. And so began the systematic persecution of people who were purported to be in cahoots with the Devil.

Why did the Church determine to stamp out the Cathars and the Manichees? The theology behind their reasoning is complex but was rooted in the idea of a 'dualism' with God on one side and the powers of evil – Satan – on the other. While the Church held that Satan was the lesser power, operating within the 'permission' granted him by God, their opponents saw God and the Devil as equals, engaged in an eternal running fight, with Mankind as the battle-ground.

Once the great machinery of the Inquisition got rolling, there was to be no stopping it. With time, it was to crush the Manichees, the Waldensians, the

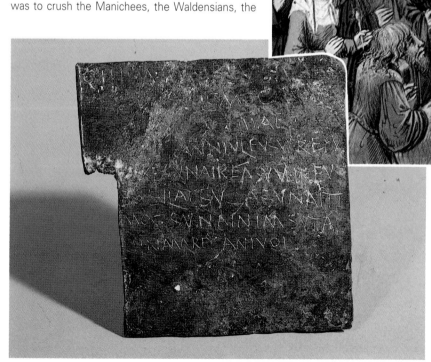

*In*Focus

A LORE UNTO THEMSELVES

A modern coven conducts an initiation ceremony, left.

Throughout the year, modern witches meet on nights of the full Moon, and gather to celebrate certain high days known as 'sabbats'. There are eight of these: May Eve (30 April), Hallowe'en (31 October), Candlemas (2 February), Lammas (1 August), the equinoxes (21 March and 21 September) and the solstices (21 June and 21 December).

A typical sabbat will involve all members of the coven, ideally 13 in number but generally between 6 and 20. Usually, the ceremonies are conducted in the nude, which means they must be performed indoors or at some isolated site.

Traditionally, the coven is led by a High Priestess as representative of the Great Goddess, but some groups have a male leader, most frequently referred to as High Priest or Magus. At the site of the sabbat, a magic circle is drawn, and a ring of witches is formed within it, hand to hand. The High Priestess, who should 'carry Phallic Wand, or Riding Pole, phallic or pine-cone tipped, if possible', enters the circle and is greeted by the senior male with the five-fold kiss on knees, genitals, breasts and lips. Then follows the ceremony of the 'drawing down of the Moon', and the initiation of new members.

The evening's ritual entertainment may conclude with the Great Rite, in which the High Priest and Priestess have sexual intercourse, either symbolically or in reality, possibly (although not usually) in front of the assembled company.

Cathars and the Knights Templar, before moving on to destroy individuals whose only crime may have been to foresee a neighbour's death in a dream. In such an environment, it was unlikely that the simple witchcraft of village 'wise' men and women could survive for long before becoming entangled with charges of heresy.

PACTS WITH THE DEVIL

Gradually, the process of trying and condemning witches became entirely divorced from ordinary law; and, in 1398, the University of Paris opened further floodgates by decreeing that any 'superstitious practice' that had results that could not 'reasonably' be accredited to God and nature had to be the result of a pact with the Devil. That, and subsequent judgements, spread terror throughout Europe: suddenly, it seemed witches and demons were everywhere, ready to strike down Christians, blight their crops, render them impotent and destroy their souls.

No doubt many of the accused actually believed themselves to be witches, and for every ten innocents tortured to extract a confession of guilt, there was probably an equal number who volunteered a confession, convinced that they were genuinely possessed by demons. Such a phenomenon is well known to modern police officers whenever a particularly sensational murder is committed: neither is it unknown for a spate of imitative crimes to follow shortly after a well-publicised killing. Likewise, 'group witchcraft' was originally the invention of the Inquisition; but it is probable that, in some isolated cases, a strong leader

could succeed in deluding a group of his or her neighbours into joining a coven for the thrill of it.

Undoubtedly there were, and still are, individuals who appear to have 'strange' powers. However, the traditional belief that they are the 'seventh child of a seventh child' is not so much a statement of fact as an indication of the comparative rarity of such people. The more down-to-earth lore associated with 'country witchcraft' today – wart curing, and knowledge of herbs and the habits of animals, for example – was widespread in a pre-industrial age, simply because people were closer to nature. They grew up knowing about the 'magic' properties of the plants that surrounded them. Today, when such skills are practised, however, they naturally smack of the truly 'occult' – in the sense of a hidden skill.

Curiously, it was a member of the Spanish Inquisition, Alonso de Salazar Frias, who in 1611 pronounced an opinion that may well have applied not only to his own time but to the myriad 'witch' cults that have spawned in Britain and the United States since the 1960s. Over a period of eight weeks, he is said to have talked to as many as 1,800 witches, many of whom had made voluntary confessions. His approach was astonishingly open-minded, and his conclusion salutary.

'Considering the above with all the Christian attention in my power, I have not found even indications from which to infer that a single act of witchcraft has really occurred... I deduce the importance of silence, and reserve from the experience that these were neither witches nor bewitched until they were talked and written about.'

THE CARDS THAT SPEAK

USING TAROT CARDS TO PREDICT FUTURE EVENTS HAS LONG BEEN ONE OF THE MOST POPULAR FORMS OF DIVINATION. BUT THE WAY IN WHICH THE CARDS ARE CONSULTED AND THE INTERPRETATION OF EACH IS VERY MUCH DEPENDENT ON THE INDIVIDUAL PRACTITIONER

In a 15th-century reading of the Tarot cards, above, a man throws up his hands after learning something unexpected. The earliest known Tarot pack dates from 1390. The cards probably originated in the East, and were spread to Europe by gypsy fortune-tellers and Moorish invaders.

Some methods of divination are aleatory – that is, they are based upon chance and involve a random selection of elements. The word 'aleatory' comes from the Latin for 'dice-player', one of the simplest divinatory methods being the throwing of dice.

However, numerous experiments in psychokinesis have suggested that an experienced dice-thrower can actually influence results; and it may well be that the subconscious mind, or some transcendental aspect of it, is able to calculate implications and select the most suitable answer to the question posed, then subconsciously causing the appropriate figure to be generated.

Some process of this kind also seems to be at work with the Tarot – probably nowadays the most popular of all divinatory methods.

The use of a pack of cards for divination is definitely not aleatory, since each of the elements selected – namely, the cards – is distinct, and has a particular significance all of its own. There are a number of packs of specially designed cards available for divination – the French firm of Grimaud, for example, markets such sets as the cards of 'Mademoiselle Le Normand', or 'The Parlour Sybil' – but some diviners are able to make do with an ordinary pack of playing cards. In this respect, it is important to remember that the Tarot pack is also an ordinary pack of playing cards. Although some of the images of the Tarot pack may appear bizarre to north-western Europeans familiar only with the standard 52-card bridge and whist pack, they do not embody any intrinsic occult significance. Indeed, for 500 years, Tarot cards have been the standard pack for a variety of common card games that go under the generic name of *tarok* or *tarocchi*.

Modern Tarot packs have 78 cards, and consist of the Minor Arcana (56 cards, divided into four suits: buttons, cups, swords and coins), and the Greater or Major Arcana (22 cards with distinctive images, each having a particular significance.) There are very many ways of 'consulting the cards', and there is no reason to suppose that any one way is more correct or successful than any other. All that is important is that the practitioner should be completely confident about his or her method and the way in which the cards are to be interpreted. Easier methods only make use of the 22 cards of the

The Tarot cards, opposite, are from the Major Arcana, and date from the 15th to early 20th century. They are 'Strength' (La Force) right and 'The Fool' (Le Fou), above right. The Major Arcana cards are numbered I-XXI: only 'The Fool' has no number, and may have been an early equivalent of the joker in today's standard pack of 52 playing cards.

Major Arcana, while more complicated methods employ all 78 cards; but even experienced practitioners often find it necessary to resort to textbooks in order to remind themselves of the accepted significance of the numbered suit cards.

The same kind of divinatory process can be carried out with a pack devoid of Major Arcana, such as a common 52-card pack, but in this case interpretation is commensurately more difficult.

There are two ways in which Tarot cards are used in divination: either a select number of cards is chosen for interpretation, or the complete pack is disposed according to a precise formula, producing a pattern of distribution in which it is the position of the card that determines its part in the divinatory process.

As in all other methods of divination, the process comprises a questioner, who asks for advice by proposing a particular question, and the diviner, who interprets the answer. The cards may be dealt out either by the questioner or by the diviner. No two authorities agree on this, and it may also depend upon the particular method employed – but it is essential that both parties should concentrate fully upon the question because a frivolous question, or one that is idly put, will provoke an answer that may be equally facetious or, possibly, quite frightening in its implications.

Cult film-maker Alejandro Jodorowsky, whose cinematic creations have included *El Topo* and *Santa Sangre,* is a dedicated reader of the Tarot. Every Wednesday, he drives from his house in Vincennes, in east Paris, to an Arab café in the rue Saint Jacques, where he gives free public readings of the cards.

The weekly event draws a large crowd, and in the space of two hours, Jodorowsky may do over 20 sittings. Like many Tarot readers, he does not predict the future. Once the shuffled cards are spread out on the table, he gives his total attention to the here-and-now problems of his enquirers, although each is allowed only one question. Around him, the café crowd listens, fascinated, to the problems aired and Jodorowsky replies. He accepts no money, but requires that the questioners merely trace the word *'merci'* (thanks) on to his palm.

The following is an example of how the Tarot cards are laid out in a pattern, and then used for divination. The questioner in this instance is a young woman, who has been married for several years. She has a full-time professional job. Due partly to the tastes and partly the ambitions of her husband, she finds herself compelled to live in a district that she finds unpleasant. Her question is whether she should she endeavour to make her present home as comfortable as possible, or whether she should try to persuade her husband to move elsewhere.

The particular arrangement of cards used is one known as the 'Celtic cross'. Only the 22 cards of the Major Arcana are required for this.

1. A card is chosen to represent the question. This is known as the significator. In this particular case, 'The Star', representing 'new beginning; pleasure; salvation', was the card selected.

2. The questioner then shuffles the remaining cards, cuts them, and places them in a pile, face down, to the left of the significator.

3. The top card of the pile is now turned over from left to right (so that it remains as it was in the pile, either upright or reversed) and placed directly on top of the significator. This card represents the present conditions in which the questioner lives or works. The card chosen happens to be 'The World' (card 1). In spite of the nature of the question asked, it therefore appears that the questioner, on the whole, feels a sense of achievement in her work, and perhaps also in her home.

4. A second card is placed across the first, to represent any immediate influences that may affect the interests of the questioner. The card in this instance is 'Temperance': in other words, whatever decision is reached, it is likely to be controlled by reason.

5. A third card is placed above the first group of cards, to represent the ultimate aim of the questioner. This turns out to be the 'Fool', reversed.

Since it is reversed, it signifies the opposite of luck or fate, and implies a rational outcome.

6. A fourth card is placed below the first group to represent influences from the past that have affected the questioner and also the question she now asks. The 'Empress' is chosen , telling us that she is a woman of considerable understanding.

7. A fifth card is placed to the right of the central group to represent the recent past. The 'Hermit' suggests that the passage of time has brought wisdom and further understanding.

8. A sixth card is placed to the left of the central group to represent influences that may come into play in the near future. The 'Hanged Man' represents adaptability and change; it brings knowledge of the future and new understanding of the past. It also advises the questioner to face up to whatever changes may come.

These first six cards drawn have presented a picture of the questioner and her problem, as well as revealing small details that she did not provide. The final four cards, placed one above the other to the right of the table, supply divinatory advice.

9. The next card represents the present position of the questioner, and may answer the question directly. 'Death', this is not to be taken literally, for it represents transformation.

10. The next card chosen represents people and factors that may have an influence upon the answer. It is the 'Wheel of Fortune' which, though also signifying change, counsels prudence.

The account book of the treasurer to Charles VI of France records a payment in the year 1392 to the painter Jacquemin Gringonneur for three packs of cards 'in gold and various colours, of several designs, for the amusement of the said King'. The three cards seen here – 'Death', left, 'The Sun', right, and 'The Fool', below right – are from 17 that survive in the Bibliothèque Nationale in Paris, and that were long believed to be the original Gringonneur cards. They are now, however, thought to be from the 15th century and of Italian origin.

*In*Focus

SIGNIFICANCE OF THE TAROT TRUMPS

1 Magician	Man in search of knowledge; the answer that he seeks
2 Woman Pope	Intuition, inspiration; subconscious memory, lack of foresight
3 Empress	Human understanding, femininity, sensuality, beauty and happiness
4 Emperor	Masculinity, independence, creativity, action
5 Pope	Advice; justice; healing
6 Lovers	Choice, decision
7 Chariot	Achievement, success; danger of defeat
8 Justice	Caution in taking advice; control of one's fate
9 Hermit	Time; wisdom; withdrawal
10 Wheel of Fortune	Change; prudence; the eternal return
11 Fortitude	Strength of purpose, coming danger
12 Hanged Man	Adaptability; desire to learn; violent change and sacrifice
13 Death	Change by transformation, rebirth
14 Temperance	Moderation, mercy; modification
15 Devil	The adversary; caution
16 The Tower	Punishment; pride; divine inspiration
17 The Star	New beginning; pleasure; salvation
18 The Moon	Uncertainty; changeability
19 The Sun	Splendour, health, wealth, affection; treachery
20 Judgement	Punishment or reward; final achievement
21 The World	Fulfilment, completion on a material level
O The Fool	Fate; luck; the end

The Tarot cards, above right, have been laid out in the spread known as the Celtic Cross. The significator (here, The Star) represents the questioner and lie in the centre of the cross, largely hidden by two other cards – The World and Temperance. Note that The Fool is reversed. The four cards to the right of the cross provide an opportunity for divinatory advice.

11. The following card chosen reveals the inner feelings of the questioner, which she may well have kept hidden. It is the Moon, reversed. This suggests very strongly that the questioner does not really want to make the change that she has said she is considering.

12. The final card represents the end result of everything indicated by the preceding cards. It is the 'Pope' – representative of the firm foundations of our lives, and concepts of natural law and justice. This card, appearing in this position, suggests that the questioner and her husband have a mutual sympathy and understanding; that their marriage appears to be a successful one; and that it would be dangerous to threaten its stability by pursuing the change that was the subject of the question.

The number of possible sequences is virtually infinite; and even if only the 22 cards of the Major Arcana are used, as in this example, there are over a thousand million million million different layouts.

THE PRACTICE OF MAGIC WAS ONCE PRIMARILY CONCERNED WITH CONJURING UP SPIRITS, SOMETIMES TO ILL-EFFECT

SYMBOLS, SIGNS AND CEREMONIES

The years from 1480 to 1680 marked the highpoint of interest in the type of ritual magic taught in the so-called *grimoires* – books of spells and magical instruction. Thereafter, there seems to have been a general decline of interest in occult ceremony: indeed, by 1800, practitioners of magical rites were few and far between. Nevertheless, a few isolated individuals had continued to experiment with methods learned from printed and manuscript *grimoires* – sometimes with surprising or unfortunate results. Typical of these experimenters was Thomas Parkes of Bristol, whose occult misadventures were recorded by the Reverend Arthur Bedford, who knew Parkes well.

Necromancy – the art of prediction through communication with the dead – once relied heavily on rituals laid down in the grimoires, medieval textbooks of magic. The magician stood in a circle inscribed with names and symbols, designed to protect him from evil demons. But things could go badly wrong, as in the case of Thomas Parkes, above, whose conjurations produced terrifying supernatural creatures that he could not control.

By trade, Parkes was a gunsmith, but he was also well-versed in mathematics, astronomy and astrology. By the latter art, he would cast horoscopes for friends and acquaintances, his prophecies often proving accurate. Nevertheless, Parkes found astrology an unsatisfactory science, for 'there was nothing in it which tended to mathematical demonstration'.

One day, the Reverend Bedford was approached by Parkes with a theological question. Was it lawful for a Christian, he asked, to raise spirits to visible appearance and converse with them? It was not, answered the clergyman.

Parkes then admitted that, using the processes outlined in a *grimoire*, the Fourth Book of Cornelius Agrippa's *Occult Philosophy,* he had been doing that very thing. He would go, he said, in the dead of night to a causeway where he drew a circle with consecrated chalk. Then, standing within the circle, 'which no spirit had power to enter', he would invoke the spirits – and they would duly appear. According to the Reverend Bedford's manuscript, these manifested themselves as follows: '... in the shape of little girls, about a foot-and-a-half [46 centimetres] high, and played about the circle. At first, he was affrighted, but after some small acquaintance this antipathy in nature wore off, and he became pleased with their company . . . they spoke with a shrill voice, like an ancient woman.'

At first, the Rev. Bedford doubted Parkes' sanity; but, after he had demonstrated the astronomical projection of a sphere, in order to prove himself free 'of the least tincture of madness', the clergyman felt compelled to accept the truth of the story. Nevertheless, he refused Parkes' offer to take him on one of his nocturnal expeditions, and sternly advised the abandonment of ritual magic.

Some three months later, Parkes once again approached the clergyman, saying he wished he had taken his advice, 'for he thought he had done that which would cost him his life'. He had decided, he said, to acquire a familiar spirit – an otherworldly being that would be continually at his service – by following the instructions given in his *grimoire*.

His first step had been to prepare a parchment book; he then went to a crossroads and invoked the spirit that was to be his familiar. The spirit duly appeared, and signed its name in the book. But then other, unwanted and uninvoked, spirits appeared, taking shapes – bears, lions, and serpents – that terrified the unhappy magician. His fears then increased, as he found it beyond his powers to control these supernatural creatures. Eventually, the spirits vanished, leaving Parkes 'in a great sweat'. The rest of the story is best told in the words of the clergyman's manuscript:

'. . . from that time he was never well so long as he lived... he expressed a hearty repentance for, and detestation of, his sins; so that though these matters cost him his life, yet I have room to believe him happy in the other world.'

Shortly after the beginning of the 19th century, there were signs of a small revival of interest in ritual magic. In 1801, for instance, Francis Barrett published a curious magical textbook, entitled *The Magus or Celestial Intelligences*. Although Barrett claimed authorship, it was largely a compilation derived from earlier *grimoires*. Barrett, who lived in what was then the London suburb of St Marylebone, was sufficiently confident of his occult abilities to advertise for pupils, and to announce the setting up of a small 'esoteric academy', the purpose of which was 'to investigate the hidden treasures of Nature'. Barrett assured prospective pupils that they would learn the secrets of natural philosophy, natural magic, the Kabbalah, chemistry, the art of making talismans, astrology and even the art of interpreting human character from facial appearance.

Whether Barrett was really competent to give practical instruction on all these subjects is uncertain; but according to the late Montague Summers, who wrote widely on witchcraft and black magic, some of Barrett's pupils 'advanced far upon the paths of transcendental wisdom'.

Throughout the course of the 19th century, small groups of English occultists studied Barrett's book and experimented with ritual magic in accordance with his instructions. One such group was centred around Frederick Hockley, a tea merchant who experimented with crystal gazing and amassed a large library of occult books and manuscripts, many of them dealing with ritual magic. Then, in the 1870s, students of the paranormal began to take an interest in the writings and ideas of the French occultist Eliphas Lévi (1810-1875). Notable among these was Kenneth Mackenzie, an active freemason who claimed to have been admitted into a secret (allegedly Rosicrucian) society. Mackenzie spent time in France and Germany, and was on friendly terms with several of the earliest members of the Golden Dawn, an organisation that taught a system of ritual magic still employed.

The Order of the Golden Dawn, a secret society whose members received successive initiations that were conferred by ceremonies bearing some resemblance to those of freemasonry, was founded

in 1888 by three masonic occultists. Of these, the most notable was S.L. MacGregor Mathers who, while at first subservient to the other two – Dr William Wynn Westcott and Dr Robert Woodman – came to dominate them in time by the sheer strength of his flamboyant personality.

PATH TO WISDOM

At first, the Golden Dawn was no more than a quasi-masonic society, and the techniques of ritual magic were not taught to its members. Nor, indeed, was any occult teaching imparted to them, save what was to be found in easily accessible books. In spite of this, newly admitted members were assured that 'the Order of the Golden Dawn, of which you have now become a member, can show you the way to much secret knowledge and spiritual progress, it can... lead... to... True Wisdom and Perfect Happiness.'

In actuality, members were far from happy and began to grumble. They wanted to practise the occult arts, particularly ritual magic, rather than just talk about them.

In 1892, Mathers decided to meet their wishes and produced a large body of instructional material that outlined a complex and – so it is claimed by those who have experimented with it – effective system of ritual magic. According to Mathers and his wife Moina, sister of the French philosopher

PHANTASMAGORIA
THIS and every EVENING,
AT THE
LYCEUM, STRAND.

Members of the Golden Dawn are seen, left, at an initiation ceremony. Originally, the society required that, as a novice's knowledge of the occult increased, he should pass through successive initiations based on the progression of the soul through the Tree of Life, illustrated below.

The top of the magic wand belonging to occultist Aleister Crowley, below left, represented the head of Janus – Roman god of beginnings – topped by a triple flame.

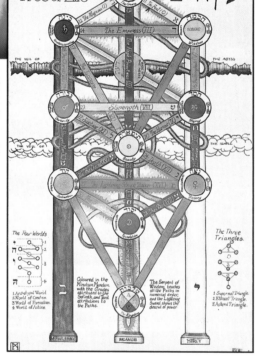

Henri Bergson, it was derived from the 'Secret Chiefs', superhuman beings of the same variety as the Mahatmas (or Masters) whom the Theosophist Madam Blavatsky claimed to represent. Mathers said he had occasionally met these beings in their physical bodies, the appointments with them being made 'astrally'. (Presumably, they either appeared to him in the course of dreams, as disembodied spirits, or perhaps he received messages telepathically from them.)

These meetings apparently exhausted Mathers. After they were over, he felt he had been in contact with a 'terrible force', found such difficulty in breathing that he compared it to being half-strangled by fumes of ether, and even suffered violent bleeding from his nose, mouth and ears.

Whether Mathers' Masters were real or imaginary, there is no doubt that the system of magical practice attributed to their teachings is intellectually coherent and, in its way, impressive. The theories behind the techniques of ritual magic taught are not only more fully developed and better expressed than they are in the writings of Eliphas Lévi, but the practice of the art is taught in a much simpler way than in the *grimoires*. (There is no ritual sacrifices of virgin rams at the dark of the Moon, for example.)

MAGICAL IMPLEMENTS

The Golden Dawn initiate who had reached the stage at which he or she received access to Mathers' instructional material began by making a set of magical implements. These, mostly made from wood, cardboard and coloured paper, included a 'Lotus Wand', signifying the 12 signs of the zodiac and the triumph of spirit over matter, a ceremonial cup – this was usually a wine glass decorated with mystic symbols – a wooden disc, symbolic of matter, and a sword, emblem of the strength and power of Mars. Once made, the implements were ceremonially consecrated.

The magician then began to devise his own ceremonies on the basis of occult knowledge. Sometimes, these were comparatively simple. Thus, for example, when a certain J.W. Brodie-Innes came to believe (on no very good grounds) that a 'vampirising entity' was obsessing himself and his wife, he burned incense on a coal from his fire and drew a pentagram in the air with his right hand, while resonantly chanting the 'name of power', *Adonai ha-Aretz* – Hebrew for 'God of the Earth'. At once, there materialised before him 'a vague blot' that soon formed itself into a terrifying apparition, a foul shape between that of 'a big bellied toad and a malicious ape'. Using the visualisation process outlined in one of Mathers' manuscripts, the magician then imagined something so strongly that it was almost perceptible to his physical sight – a glowing ball of fiery force which he directed against the obsessing entity. There was 'a slight shock, a foul smell, a momentary dimness, and then the thing was gone'.

POWER OF SYMBOLS

Rather more elaborate rituals – those, for example, for raising spirits and the 'making of an astral shroud of darkness' (that is, obtaining invisibility) – were also undertaken. The basic form of these was taken from the *grimoires*, but the ceremonies were enriched by the incorporation into them of additional material derived from the symbol system of correspondences that Mathers claimed to have derived from his teachers. A snake, for example, was said to correspond to both the god and the planet Mercury; so, if a Golden Dawn magician were evoking spirits whose nature was mercurial, he might incorporate snake fat into the candles employed in the ceremony.

The Golden Dawn eventually collapsed into a number of competing schisms. Personality differences in time destroyed even these; but the ritual magic of the Golden Dawn survived. Even today, in both the UK and North America, groups and isolated individuals practising Golden Dawn magic are to be found in almost every large city.

CELESTIAL HARMONIES

THE SYMBOLISM USED IN THE CONSTRUCTION OF RELIGIOUS BUILDINGS IS BASED, IN GENERAL, ON VARIOUS SYSTEMS OF SACRED GEOMETRY. WHAT SORT OF SECRET LANGUAGE IS INVOLVED?

Among the Hopi Indian tribe of North America, the timing of many religious ceremonies is determined by the alignment of the stars. At particular seasons of the year, the priests and chosen members of the tribe descend into underground chambers, known as *kivas*, and watch the passage of the stars through the entrance slit. Rituals are performed during the time that it takes the relevant constellation to pass overhead. The duration of the entire ceremony, as well as its timing, is thus determined by astronomical – and astrological – conditions.

This megalithic tomb at Maes Howe, Orkney, was carefully aligned so that the setting Sun would shine down the long entrance passage only at the winter solstice. Christianity also aligned its buildings by the Sun, and assimilated other pagan practices. The painting, by an unknown 16th-century artist, of St. Géneviève sitting in a megalithic stone circle, below, dramatically illustrates the blending of Christian and pagan elements.

The precise motives of the megalith-builders in Europe have been the subject of much conjecture, but it seems reasonable to suppose that the megalithic monuments were constructed for a similar purpose. The stars were certainly studied for practical reasons in ancient societies, and not merely for the timing of religious ceremonies. In ancient Babylonia, for example, the time for sowing crops was the 40 days during which the Pleiades were invisible. And research in Britain by, among others, Sir Norman Lockyer and Professor Alexander Thom suggests strongly that megalithic monuments are subtly aligned to form observatories from which the movement of the stars could be accurately charted.

The Christian missionaries who evangelised Britain during the seventh and eighth centuries found a country of heathens who worshipped a confused pantheon – a mixture of Celtic and Roman gods and deities of more ancient origin. The missionaries, therefore, feared that their Christian God would be adopted as just one more divinity on a level with all the others. Indeed, many Christian feasts and rituals were taken from, and celebrated as thinly disguised versions of, pagan counterparts. Moreover, well into the medieval period, pre-Christian festivals at the equinoxes or solstices were celebrated with dancing in churches or churchyards. These were often led – despite repeated injunctions by higher Church authorities – by the priests themselves.

The custom of dancing at ancient sacred sites marked by megalithic monuments also persisted,

much to the dismay of the Church, which regarded the continuance of pagan religious practices as a direct threat. It was in order to stamp them out that churches were often built on the very sites of ancient pagan monuments. Indeed, they were frequently dedicated to St George or St Michael, both of whom were dragon-slayers – the dragon being the symbol of the 'old religion'.

But even though churches were built on ancient sacred sites to eradicate pagan influences, church architecture, curiously enough, preserved at least one pagan element – the practice of precise astronomical alignment. Following the ancient tradition of the sacred geometry of the temples of Greece and Egypt, churches were built on an axis that pointed in the precise direction of sunrise on the morning of the feast-day of the saint to whom the church was dedicated. When this axis had been determined, the master mason and his assistants would lay out the foundations of the church using a knotted cord, just as their ancient Egyptian counterparts had done.

Medieval churches were also designed to harmonise with the world as medieval Man perceived it. As Nigel Pennick remarks in *Sacred Geometry:*

Two members of the warlike order of Knights Templar are dressed for battle in the 18th-century engraving, left. The Templars built churches with a circular plan, intended to represent the physical universe of material forces, but this was eventually condemned as heretical.

The 13th-century Templar chapel, below, at Vera Cruz, Segovia, Spain, is also round.

*In*Focus

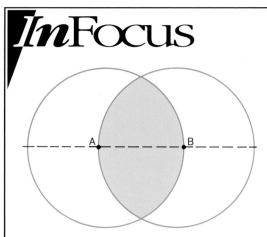

MEDIEVAL MOTIF

The sacred symbol of the *vesica piscis* (literally 'fish's bladder') is a crucial motif in medieval churches throughout Europe (as in the 12th-century decoration of a reliquary at Limoges, France, *above right*). The shape is formed by the intersection of two circles of equal radius, the centre of each lying on the circumference of the other, as *above*. Using the *vesica piscis,* it is possible to construct – with only a ruler and compasses – all the regular figures of plane geometry, and so the figure was extensively used in the laying out of sacred buildings.

Perhaps because of this, the *vesica piscis* is seen as the symbol of creation and regeneration – and has even in certain cultures represented the genitals of the Mother Goddess, from whom all physical life is believed by some to spring.

The Christian Church, meanwhile, has regarded the *vesica piscis* as a symbol of Christ, because of its fish shape, which was used by early Christians as a secret sign for Christ. The symbolism is reinforced by the overlapping circles that compose the figure: Christ is seen as the meeting point of heaven and earth, spiritual and material, creator and created.

'Physical manifestations of the *summa theologiae,* the microcosmic embodiment of the created universe, cathedrals in their perfect completed form, united in their position, orientation, geometry, proportion and symbolism, attempt to create the Great Work – the unification of man with God.'

True enough, the physical fabric of the church was, to the educated medieval mind, a rich metaphor of the world as organised religion taught Man to see it. The traditional nave-and-transepts of most churches reflected the fundamental symbol of Christianity – the Latin cross. It also represented the human form. The French theologian Durandus of St Pourcain (c. 1270-1334) wrote in *Rationale Divinorum Officiorum* ('Explanation of the Divine Office'):

'The arrangement of a material church resembles that of the human body; the chancel... represents the head, the transepts, the hands and arms, and the remainder – towards the west – the rest of the body. The sacrifice of the altar denotes the vows of the heart.'

By the Renaissance, architectural theorists were using similar arguments to insist that the only correct form for church design was the nave-and-transepts plan. Among them was Pietro Cataneo who argued, in *I Quattro Libri dell' Architettura* ('The Four Books of Architecture'), published in 1554, that the temple was symbolic of the body of God, and that churches should also celebrate the crucified Christ and therefore take the shape of the cross. Thus, the church would represent both the body of Man (made in the image of God) and the crucifixion of Christ.

A separate, but parallel, tradition of building round churches came to be regarded, in consequence, as heretical. These churches represent the *imago mundi* (image of the world), and they hold a special place in Christian architecture. It was, in fact, the round form that was chosen for the Church of the Holy Sepulchre in Jerusalem, which marked the tomb of Christ and (so it was believed) the centre of the world.

In the late medieval period, round churches also became associated with the fabulously wealthy military order of the Knights Templar. When the order was brutally suppressed in 1312, its members were accused of numerous heresies – such as blasphemy – and their form of church-building, too, was branded as heretical.

Unlike the nave-and-transepts design, the round form did not represent the body of a man, the body of God, or the cross on which Christ was crucified. It represented, instead, the physical universe – the domain of material and ungodly forces. The Templars believed that the place of God in the Universe had been usurped by his evil counterpart, the *rex mundi* ('king of the world'), and that these two waged an incessant battle over men's souls, in which it was by no means certain that good would win. At the centre of Templar churches stood an altar in the form of a perfect cube, symbol of the Earth within the heavens.

With the suppression of the Templars, the building of round churches virtually ceased until Renaissance architects reintroduced the form, following their study of certain classical temples.

The cruciform plan of Chartres cathedral, in France, left, symbolises both the crucifixion of Christ and the body of Man, made in the image of God.

But it was soon suppressed again by Church authorities, on the grounds that pagan designs should not be used for Christian buildings.

That sacred symbolism of this kind was taken very seriously is clear. Indeed, medieval churches abounded with paintings and statuary in which more geometrical symbolism was to be found. The circle, for example, was the symbol of the infinite Universe – the cosmos; the square represented the microcosm, the finite Earth; the triangle stood for the Holy Trinity – Father, Son and Holy Ghost. In medieval art, the shape of the *vesica piscis* (literally, 'fish's bladder') also had a complex symbolism.

In addition to these, there were several systems of proportions that, although commonly used in classical and medieval times, did not become fully articulated until the Renaissance. Chief among these were the proportions defined by a triangle with sides measuring three, four and five units. This derived from the surveying instrument used by the ancient Egyptians, and the so-called Golden Section, known since the time of the ancient Greek mathemetician, Euclid. To see just how far such use of proportion can be taken, it is interesting to consider a document describing the design of the church of San Francesco della Vigna in Venice, Italy. The church was begun in 1534, under the direction

Little remains of the fourth-century BC marble rotunda in the sanctuary of Athena Pronaia at Delphi, above; but of its original 20 Doric columns, three have been re-erected. It was classical Greek buildings such as this that inspired the Renaissance architects to revive the round form in church architecture. Bramante's little Tempietto church in Rome (completed in 1502), above right, exhibits many such classical features.

of the architect Jacopo Sansovino. But arguments had arisen over the proportional system suitable for such a building, and a Franciscan monk, named Francesco di Giorgi, was called in to advise.

Giorgi suggested a system of proportion based on the number three – symbolic of the Trinity. His overall system was also related to the proportions of Vitruvian Man – the ideally shaped human devised by the ancient Roman engineer and architect, Vitruvius. Heavily symbolic and rigorously proportional, this design system was approved by the painter Titian, the architect Serlio, and the humanist philosopher Fortunio Spira. The facade of the church was completed 30 years later by Palladio, who used the very same system of proportion.

The ancient tradition of sacred geometry can be read as an attempt to make the buildings of Man harmonise with the world in which he finds himself, and to be physical expressions of fundamental truths, both temporal and eternal. Sacred geometry has an explicit foundation in the natural world. As the preamble to Nigel Pennick's *Sacred Geometry* puts it: 'Geometry underlies the structure of all things – from galaxies to molecules. Each time a geometrical form is created, an expression of this universal oneness is made... Sacred geometry is responsible for the feeling of awe generated by a Gothic cathedral as well as for the "rightness" of a Georgian drawing-room.'

Examples cited to support this include the beautiful double-helix of the DNA (deoxyribonucleic acid) molecule; the manifestation of the logarithmic spiral (based ultimately upon the golden ratio) in the shell of the nautilus mollusc; and the harmonic intervals (similar to those in music) in atomic energy levels. All these seem to be manifestations of a transcendent geometrical order. This belief has yet to be proved by science; but what is beyond doubt is the beauty of the material language it has generated.

The Venetian church of San Francesco della Vigna, seen above in a painting by Canaletto (1697-1768), was based on the classical proportions of Vitruvian Man.

An 18th-century church mural of the Trinity, from Bulgaria, **left,** *shows the Father, Son and Holy Ghost (represented by a dove) within a circle – the symbol of the cosmos. The square represents the finite Earth within the cosmos.*

" WHEN FIFTEENTH-CENTURY WRITERS SPOKE OF DERIVING ARCHITECTURAL FORMS FROM THE HUMAN BODY, THEY DID NOT THINK OF THE BODY AS A LIVING ORGANISM, BUT AS A MICROCOSM *"* OF THE UNIVERSE...

JAMES S. ACKERMAN, THE ARCHITECTURE OF MICHELANGELO

PERSPECTIVES

THE CANDLESTICK OF FAITH

While religious symbolism permeates much of Christian art and architecture, the far older religion of Judaism has its own objects of symbolic importance. One of the central motifs of Judaism is the menorah – the seven-branched candlestick that was originally made for the Tabernacle (holy sanctuary) of the desert-dwelling Hebrews. This menorah was eventually placed in Solomon's Temple at Jerusalem, and its successor vanished with the destruction of the Second Temple in AD 70.

Since then, the menorah – in both its seven- and eight-branched forms – has come to embody for Jews not only the memory of the Temples' destruction, but Messianic hope, as well as personal and national redemption. The very shape of the menorah also has meaning: it is thought to represent the sacred Tree of Life – a common metaphor in Jewish tradition. According to rabbinical literature, the seven lights also represent the seven days of Creation.

After the loss of the Temple menorah, rabbinic law prevented Jews from making copies of the original for ritual use. It was only in the 12th century that Jews began to use menorahs in the synagogue and the home, especially over Chanukah, the Festival of Lights. (It was for this festival that the eight-branched version was developed, with the central, or ninth, light used to kindle the others, as pictured here.) Today, the menorah is one of the most popular images of Jewish art and religion – a symbol of everlasting light, hope and faith.

THE GLASTONBURY LEGEND

GLASTONBURY IS A MECCA FOR VISITORS INTRIGUED BY ITS LINKS WITH PAGANISM, EARLY CHRISTIANITY, KING ARTHUR AND THE HOLY GRAIL. WHAT IS KNOWN ABOUT ITS DISTANT PAST?

The Holy Grail, seen right in a detail from a Rhenish glass panel, is a fundamental part of the tales that help imbue Glastonbury, below, with an aura of romance and mystery. The legendary vessel is linked with Joseph of Arimathea and also King Arthur, who both have strong Glastonbury connections.

For some people, the English market town of Glastonbury, on the river Brue in Somerset, is just another historic place to visit. For others, however, it exerts a strange, powerful and disturbing force. As Anthony Roberts writes in the foreword to the book *Glastonbury: Ancient Avalon, New Jerusalem*:

'Glastonbury is one of those highly charged sacred focal points for the generation and transmission of cosmic energies. It is a planetary beacon and powerhouse of the spirit that enlightens all who approach its mysteries with a sense of humble participation and genuine love. It is a dangerous place because of the very potency of its spiritual energies, as those who have despoiled its brooding aura have discovered to their cost. It can generate madness and death as easily as it can produce tranquility and revelation.'

Described in one guide to Somerset as a 'town of mean streets and commonplace houses', Glastonbury nevertheless draws thousands of tourists every year. So what is the attraction? Among the claims made for Glastonbury are that it

According to this tradition, it was Jesus who built the Old Church, afterwards spending several years at Glastonbury with Druid priests who lived in a small community on top of the Tor.

Joseph of Arimathea is a minor but significant biblical character. A wealthy member of the Jerusalem town council, he was said to be a secret disciple of Jesus. Whatever his religion, it was he who arranged for Jesus to be taken down from the cross and buried in the new tomb he had prepared for himself. Thereafter, Joseph disappears from *The Bible*, but his story was picked up in the *Gospel of Nicodemus*, also known as the *Acts of Pilate*, which is included in the collection of writings known as the *Apocryphal New Testament*.

From Nicodemus, we learn the unauthenticated tale that, following the crucifixion, Joseph of Arimathea was imprisoned by the Jews and then led to freedom by the risen Christ. This theme was developed in about 1200 by a Burgundian knight, named Robert de Boron, in a long poem called *Joseph di Arimathie*. Here, Joseph is presented with a 'vessel' – often portrayed as a cup used by Jesus at the Last Supper and in which his blood was collected as he hung on the cross. This vessel,

was the religious centre of pagan Britain; that it was visited by the boy Jesus; that Joseph of Arimathea brought the Holy Grail here and founded the first Christian settlement in Britain; that Christian hermits already here were organised by St Patrick into a formal community; that King Arthur was buried here; that a ritual maze is traceable on the Tor; and that, several thousand years ago, people shaped the whole Glastonbury terrain into a zodiac.

FIRST BRITISH CHURCH

What truth, if any, lies behind these confusing and conflicting claims? At the centre of many of the legends is the now ruined abbey and the Old Church, a small building of wattle and daub that pre-dated the abbey on the same site. It was the Old Church that, in fact, introduced Joseph of Arimathea into Glastonbury folklore. According to one tradition, it was Joseph who built the church – the first Christian foundation in Britain – and who dedicated it to the Virgin Mary.

There are several versions of Joseph's journey to Britain. In one, he arrived at Somerset with 11 companions and was made welcome by a local king, Arviragus. This king then made him a substantial grant of land at Glastonbury on which to establish a religious community. On the way there, the missionaries, weary from long travels, stopped to rest on the summit of nearby Wearyall Hill. Joseph, it is said, thrust his staff into the ground and, through a miracle, it sprouted into a thorn tree that thereafter blossomed every Christmas Day. The original tree was later destroyed, but its descendants still thrive today, blossoming in January since the changeover to the Gregorian calendar in the mid-18th century.

Another version claims that, in AD 63, Joseph was sent to Britain by the Apostle James, who was at that time preaching in western Europe. A third variation says that Joseph was sent by St James because he was already familiar with the land, having accompanied the boy Jesus on a visit to Britain.

The site of Glastonbury Abbey, above, is said to be the same as that of the first Christian church in Britain, founded by Joseph of Arimathea, right. The Holy Thorn, below, a unique hawthorn first found in Glastonbury, is supposed to have sprung up miraculously when Joseph's staff was thrust in the ground.

or Holy Grail, was eventually entrusted to one of Joseph's followers, Peter, and taken to the 'vales of Avaron' [Avalon] in 'the far West'. Many people believe that this means Glastonbury in England; and in subsequent romances, it became Joseph himself who brought the Grail to Britain.

But Joseph of Arimathea does not appear in any of the writings or chronicles about Glastonbury before the last decade or so of the 12th century. No connection between the two, for instance, is made in a history of the abbey written in about 1130 by William of Malmesbury, a highly respected historian who took considerable pains to ensure the accuracy of his material. William believed the Old Church to be of great antiquity, but did not think it had been constructed in the lifetime of the Apostles.

MEDDLING MONKS

In 1184, there was a raging fire at Glastonbury that destroyed the Old Church and many of the abbey's documents, records and holy relics. The monks then launched what amounted to a publicity campaign to attract pilgrims – and money – to the abbey. Part of their programme was to produce a new edition of William's history, and it was the unknown editor of this work who made the link between Joseph and the Apostle James, asserting that St James had sent Joseph to Britain. He quoted as his source a bishop of Lisieux, France, named Freculf. Turning to Freculf, we find that, while he certainly claimed that St James was evangelising in western Europe in the first century, he did not mention Joseph of Arimathea, nor any journey to Britain in or around AD 63.

Nobody knows exactly when Christianity reached Britain. But whenever that may have been, Glastonbury is one of the places where it might well have begun. Why, though, should this be?

Many economic historians have stressed Glastonbury's importance as a trade centre with Gaul and the Mediterranean. This being so, there is no inherent reason why a party of Christian missionaries should not have followed the trade routes, as

Modern Glastonbury, above, is a rather ordinary market town in Somerset. Yet it draws thousands of tourists every year – visitors who look beyond the 'mean streets and commonplace houses' to the Tor, below. This, just outside the town, is the source of many interesting conjectures about Glastonbury's special power of attraction.
The aerial view of Glastonbury Tor, below right, shows the terraces on its slopes, thought by some once to have been a three-dimensional maze of occult significance.

they so often did elsewhere, arriving in Glastonbury. So perhaps the legend of Joseph of Arimathea, like so many tales based on oral tradition, does contain a kernel of truth, after all.

It is harder, though, to credit the story of the miracle of the thorn tree, which is supposed to have sprung from Joseph's staff. Yet, there is another aspect to the Holy Thorn. The tree is botanically interesting, being a freak variety of hawthorn that can be propagated only by grafting. This is the kind of knowledge that may have been exclusive to the Glastonbury monks, and it may have given the tree a special significance. It is also possible that the timing of the flowering at Christmas may in turn have inspired the monks to attach a Christian connotation to the plant. Another suggestion is that the thorn was the focus of some pagan act of worship, and that the monks gave it Christian significance in order to weaken the attraction of paganism.

Paganism also lays its own claims to Glastonbury. Indeed, if an important pagan holy place did exist there, it would explain the establishment of an early Christian settlement there, too. It

was not uncommon for the Church to take over existing sacred sites and Christianise them.

Glastonbury Tor is the most impressive landmark in the region. It rises 500 feet (150 metres) out of the flat Somerset countryside and is visible from all directions for up to 20 miles (30 kilometres). There is a belief that the Tor was built by ancient peoples, but it is in fact a natural feature. The summit, which is fairly flat, is about 100 by 50 feet (30 by 15 metres). On the slopes are numerous terraces, which are conventionally explained as either natural or the result of a prehistoric system of agriculture that left ridges or lynchets on the terrain. To these theories has been added one of an occult nature by Geoffrey Russell, who has suggested that they are the remains of a three-dimensional maze that symbolically represented the road from hell – the base of the Tor – to heaven, the summit. This maze, he proposed, was walked by early Christian pilgrims and also possibly followed leys. He also put forward the view that crossing the lines to get to the top of the Tor could be dangerous. Francis Hitching, in his book *Earth Magic*, seems to support this idea when he says that many modern tourists who have climbed the Tor, crossing the maze in the process, claim to have experienced an inexplicable drain of energy.

The possibility of a pagan religious settlement is supported by the evidence of two graves in which bodies have the heads pointing to the south – generally a non-Christian alignment. But little else points to a religious community.

This leaves the possibility of a defensive or quasi-military settlement. The Tor certainly com-

Pilgrims, such as those illustrated above, were very important to medieval Church finances because they spent freely. So when William of Malmesbury's popular work on Glastonbury Abbey was burned in 1184, the monks produced a new edition. It was only then that Joseph of Arimathea entered the Glastonbury story.

mands an unparalleled view of the surrounding countryside, and difficulty of access, of course, would work in favour of easy defence.

The Life of St Gildas – a book written in around 1150 – is particularly interesting in its application to Glastonbury because it tells how Melwas kidnapped Guinevere, the wife of King Arthur, and held her at Glastonbury. Arthur arrived with his army to rescue her, but bloodshed was averted by the intervention of Gildas, whose mediation restored Guinevere to Arthur. If Melwas did kidnap Arthur's wife, he would have wanted to keep her somewhere he could defend. So why not a stronghold on Glastonbury Tor?

It is impossible to discuss the early history of Glastonbury without mentioning Arthur. But it is almost impossible to distinguish fact from fiction. In the *Historia Regum Britanniae* ('History of the Kings of Britain'), written in about 1136 and now regarded as largely fictional, Geoffrey of Monmouth tells us of the death of Arthur. According to his account, Arthur's traitorous nephew Mordred seized the kingdom of Britain while the king was abroad. Arthur returned to Britain with his army and drove Mordred and his mercenary army into Cornwall, where the two forces met in a final, terrible battle near the river Camblan. Mordred was killed. 'Arthur himself,' says Geoffrey, 'our renowned king, was mortally wounded and was carried off to the Isle of Avalon, so that his wounds might be attended to... this in the year 542... '

But where was Avalon? Geoffrey of Monmouth does not give a hint of where it was located in his *Historia,* but it seems unlikely that he had Somerset in mind. In his poem *Vita Merlin* ('The Life of Merlin'), written in about 1148, he also speaks of Avalon in terms that are not compatible with Somerset. William of Malmesbury, a more trustworthy historian, is in fact quite specific in saying that the location of Arthur's grave was unknown. Yet, 40 years after these two were writing, Avalon was being identified as Glastonbury, as if the connection were an ancient tradition. Moreover, the monks at Glastonbury Abbey claimed to have located Arthur's very grave at this fascinating site.

LEGIONS OF HELL

THE NAZI PARTY'S RISE TO POWER HAS OFTEN BEEN ATTRIBUTED TO OCCULT PRACTICE. ADOLF HITLER HIMSELF WAS UNDOUBTEDLY FASCINATED BY THE 'BLACK ARTS'. HOW AND WHY DID THIS SOMEWHAT BIZARRE ASSOCIATION DEVELOP?

The swastika became the official insignia of the Nazi Party, as shown below on banners at a rally at Nuremberg in 1933. Sitting on a white disc with a red background, it was a striking symbol which to Adolf Hitler, right, represented all the ideals of the Nationalist movement. Many have seen Hitler's decision to reverse the ancient symbol – to use a 'lefthanded' swastika rather than the traditional 'right-handed' one – as an indication of his sinister leanings. Once a symbol of good fortune, the swastika is now seen throughout the world as the embodiment of evil itself.

I n the late summer of 1940, as the Battle of Britain was drawing to its close, Toby O'Brien, press secretary to Winston Churchill, suddenly had an inspiration. He was sitting in his bath one morning, when the words of a coarse comic song began to form, 'unbidden', in his mind. He repeated his composition over lunch later that day to a group of high-ranking British officers in Whitehall. They were convulsed with mirth. Some of them wrote it down, while others memorised it. Within weeks, it

had filtered through the ranks and was on the lips of squadron leaders, squaddies and admirals. Sung to the tune of *Colonel Bogey* it went:

'Hitler, he only had one ball;
Goring had two but very small.
Himmler was very similar,
But poor old Goebbels
Had no balls at all.'

Toby O'Brien certainly did not believe his composition was accurate: precious little was known about the sexual endowments or habits of the Führer. But when Russian military surgeons examined Hitler's charred remains in the Berlin bunker in May 1945, they discovered that Hitler was indeed monorchid – that is, he possessed but one testicle. It was a bizarre and extreme coincidence.

Hitler's defect may indeed have had a profound significance for the development of his occult ideas. According to Dr Walter Stein, whose observations on personal conversations with Hitler in Vienna formed the basis of Trevor Ravenscroft's *The Spear of Destiny*, Hitler had formed, as early as 1912, a passion for the music of Richard Wagner – particularly for *Parsifal,* which praised Teutonic knighthood and exalted the Aryan race. Soon, Hitler discovered Wagner's source: the medieval poetry of Wolfram von Eschenbach. In fact, it was through buying a copy of Eschenbach's *Parsival* that had once belonged to Hitler that Stein met him. Dr Stein was impressed by the meticulousness of the marginal notes, though he was simultaneously appalled by

Toby O Brien, below, penned an unwittingly accurate lampoon against Hitler in 1940.

Long before Guido von List, below, adopted the swastika as the emblem of his neo-pagan movement in Germany in the late 19th century, the 'crooked cross' was a widespread symbol of good luck, of life and of energy. The swastikas on the figure, right, part of the handle of a bucket found in the 9th-century ship-burial at Oseberg, Norway, represent the hammers of Thor, god of thunder and war. Those on the plinth of the statue of Kali, above right, meanwhile, signify a life-giving, regenerative force.

the pathological race-hatred that they showed. Among them, there appeared numerous references to the character Klingsor, whom Hitler apparently identified with the notorious ninth-century tyrant, Landulph II of Capua.

Landulph's avaricious grasping for power had led him to study the black arts, and it was for these practices that he was excommunicated in AD 875. But one other fact must have given Hitler a sense of identity with the ninth-century 'Führer'. Landulph seems to have been either partly or totally castrated: Eschenbach described him as 'the man who was smooth between the legs'.

We know that Hitler was easily influenced as a youth, avidly soaking up the ideas of those –

Wagner and Nietzsche, for instance – who impressed him. Landulph's power mania and the unfortunate anatomical similarity to himself must have struck the young Adolf, and there is reason to suspect that Landulph's black magic did so, too. There is also evidence that Hitler was impressed by magical symbolism from the beginning of his political career.

PAGAN RITES

Throughout the latter half of the 19th century, German pseudo-intellectual circles had been obsessed with a movement compounded of pagan ritual and notions of Nordic purity invented by a man named Guido von List. Born in 1848, the son of a rich trader in leather goods and boots – pointers, perhaps, to things to come – von List had renounced his Catholicism when he was 14 with a solemn oath that he would one day build a temple to Woden (or Odin), the war god of Scandinavian mythology.

By the 1870s, von List had a sizeable group of followers, dedicated to observing pagan feasts at the solstices and equinoxes. In 1875, they attracted attention to themselves by worshipping the Sun as Baldur, the Nordic god, slain in battle, who rose from the dead. The rite was held on a hilltop near Vienna, and concluded with von List burying eight wine bottles that were carefully laid out in the shape of a swastika.

The swastika had been a widespread symbol of good fortune from earliest times and among all nations: it had been found on Chinese, Mongolian and American Indian artifacts, was used by the ancient Greeks as a pottery decoration, and by medieval architects as a border design for stained

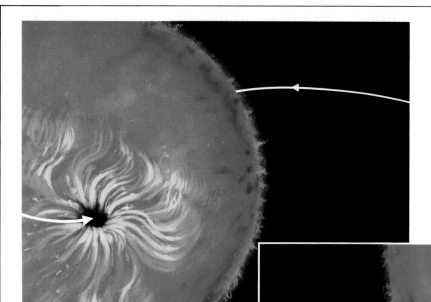

Hörbiger's belief that planets follow a spiral path led him to suggest that there were originally four moons orbiting the Earth, of which our present Moon is the only remaining one. The last collision of a moon with the Earth, some 13,000 years ago, he claimed, caused the disappearance of Atlantis – which the Nazis believed to be the original Aryan homeland.

Himmler was particularly impressed with Hörbiger's theories, and declared that he would build an observatory in Linz, his home town, dedicated to Copernicus, Kepler – and Hörbiger.

*In*Focus

A WORLD OF ICE

How did the cosmological theories of a blacksmith-turned-engineer become a mainstay of the Nazi world view?

The man in question was Hanns Hörbiger (1860-1931), *far right,* who believed that, among the 'cosmic building stuff' making up the Universe, there exists water in its 'cosmic form' – ice. This ice, he said, forms itself into large blocks that orbit young stars. Ignoring Kepler's laws of motion, which state that orbiting bodies travel in ellipses, Hörbiger argued that these blocks of ice follow a spiral path, so that they eventually collide with the star, *above,* causing an enormous explosion. The star then ejects a molten mass of rotating matter, *above right,* which forms a new solar system, *right.*

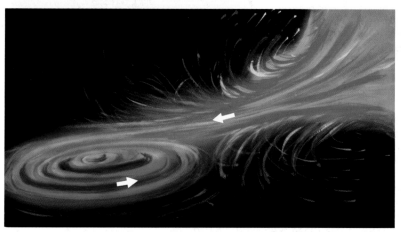

glass windows. Its name in Middle English, *fylfot,* means 'fill foot', since it was a device used for 'filling the foot' of windows. 'Swastika' stems from the Sanskrit *Su asti,* which means, literally translated, 'Good, he is'. In fact, the swastika, with its arms trailing as if the pattern were spinning clockwise, symbolised the Sun and the power of light.

In the 1920s, when the National Socialist movement was still in its infancy, Hitler asked for designs to be submitted for an easily recognisable symbol, akin to the hammer and sickle of the Russian communists. Friedrich Krohn, a dentist who was also an occultist, suggested a swastika on a white disc with a red background – red for blood and the social ideal, white for nationalism and purity of race, and the swastika for 'the struggle for victory of Aryan man'.

Hitler was delighted but for one detail – the traditional 'right-handed' swastika was to be reversed to form what the writer Francis King terms 'an evocation of evil, spiritual devolution and black magic'.

Dr Krohn fully realised Hitler's intention in changing the ancient sign, for he was a member of the *Germanenorden* – German Order – which, with the Thule Society, had taken over where von List's rather amateurish organisation had left off in the years before the First World War. Both societies, which eventually became almost interchangeable in ideas and even membership, were originally composed of the German officer class and professions, who were convinced of a massive international Jewish conspiracy, backed up by occult practices. To counter this, they established their own Nordic occult-based freemasonry, complete with elaborate rituals and robes, Viking helmets and swords. More importantly, the Thule Society – which took its name from the fabled land of Ultima Thule, a sort of paradise on Earth – began to recruit new members from the lower classes and disseminated anti-Semitic material in its various newspapers. One of these, the *Völkischer Beobachter*, eventually became the official journal of the Nazi Party.

There is no doubt that Hitler, both in his down-and-out days in Vienna and later, as leader of the rising Nazi Party in the 1920s, was constantly fascinated by fringe occult theories. One of these was the lunatic 'World Ice Theory', a complicated set of ideas propagated by an Austrian engineer named Hanns Hörbiger (1860-1931). He held that the planets had been created by the collision of stars, such as our Sun, with huge chunks of ice. Hörbiger also held that his system enabled him to forecast the weather accurately. Some occult writers, notably Pauwels and Bergier in their *Dawn of Magic*, have even suggested that Hörbiger's forecasts influenced Hitler's disastrous Russian campaign.

Latterly, Hitler became obsessed with map dowsing – swinging a pendulum over a map to find hidden objects. The topic was brought to the attention of Hitler's aides by an architect named Ludwig Straniak, yet another amateur occultist. Straniak demonstrated to German naval officers his apparent ability to pinpoint the whereabouts of their ships at sea, simply by dangling a pendulum over an admiralty chart. They were particularly impressed when he located the pocket battleship *Prinz Eugen*, at that time on a secret mission.

THE BLACK MAGICIANS

Hitler's involvement with astrology, and prediction in general, has been much debated. It has even been claimed that he had powers of precognition, which allowed him to foresee the lack of opposition to his invasions of Austria and Czechoslovakia. But Hitler's real talent was as a masterly judge of the European political mood – an intuition that deserted him when he decided to invade Poland in 1939.

Josef Goebbels, propaganda minister, used astrology cleverly but cynically – quoting Nostradamus, for instance, in support of Nazi domination. Hitler and, in particular, SS chief Himmler took astrology seriously.

In view of this varied preoccupation with the occult, many have suggested that, among high-ranking Nazis, Hitler and Himmler at least were in a real sense 'black magicians'. However, one great question confronts those who claim this. Why,

❚❚ LIKE A SHAMAN, HE [HITLER]

HAD EYES OF FIRE AND THE FACULTY

OF CONJURING UP THE SPIRITS

FROM WITHIN THE ABYSS OF HIS

OWN SOUL. ❚❚

CHRISTOPHER NUGENT,

MASKS OF SATAN

The German pocket battleship Prinz Eugen, top, was located by occultist Ludwig Straniak, simply by swinging a pendulum over a map. After hearing of Straniak's impressive demonstrations, Hitler himself became interested in – and then obsessed with – map dowsing.

Although no believer in the occult, Josef Goebbels, above, minister for propaganda and enlightenment, recognised Hitler's fascination for the subject and skilfully used it as a psychological weapon to further the Nazi cause among the German people.

when the Nazis rose to power, were occult writings and practices so rigorously stamped upon?

In 1934, a first move was made when the Berlin police issued a ban on all forms of fortune-telling, from fairground palmists to society astrologers. That the orders came from central headquarters is certain, and the officers who carried out the orders were very confused as to the intention behind them.

Next came a general suppression of all occult groups, even – to the chagrin and surprise of members – the German Order and the Thule Society. Both contained many Nazis, of course, but even for these there was no exemption. For instance, Jörg Lanz von Liebenfels, whose writings inspired much of the German racial mystique, and who boasted that by introducing Hitler to occult groups he had been his guru, was told that he must not publish occult works in future.

With the sole exceptions of 'inner party members', such as certain of Himmler's personal SS aides, occultists of all shades had been done away with or driven underground in German-occupied countries by 1940.

An answer to the enigma has been mooted by such writers as Francis King and J. H. Brennan. They argue that in regimes that in some ways are analogous with Hitler's – Mao's China, for instance, and Stalin's Russia – there was no such systematic weeding out of occultists. True, Stalin pounced on freemasons and the like, but only because they belonged to 'secret societies' *per se*, not because of their supposed magical activities. In China, even after the Cultural Revolution, seers and astrologers were frowned upon as superstitious, but nothing desperate was done against them. They were more mocked at than persecuted. Intriguingly, it seems authoritarian regimes do not usually fear magical practices as such.

But Nazi Germany had to trample down 'freelance' occultists, because it was in effect trampling down its own rivals. There was, in fact, only one occult movement permissible under the Third Reich, and it was hidden deep in its coils. It was led by the supreme magus, Adolf Hitler, and his acolyte, Heinrich Himmler – both of them known to have been powerful black magicians.

EXORCISM HAS BEEN PART OF CHRISTIANITY SINCE ITS EARLIEST DAYS. ITS EFFICACY MAY BE QUESTIONED, BUT THE RITUAL INVOLVED CAN, IT SEEMS, BRING COMFORT TO UNFORTUNATE VICTIMS OF POLTERGEIST PHENOMENA

A mong those victims of poltergeist activity who plead for, or even demand, an exorcism – and to judge from figures quoted by leading exorcists there are many hundreds – few initially have any idea at all of what is involved. Even fewer are suitable for such a rite. Indeed, there is agreement among those who have been concerned with poltergeists that only about two per cent of all reported cases genuinely involve inexplicable phenomena – that is, psychokinetic effects for which no cause can be found. But while there may be no explanation for the means whereby mattresses are slashed, or the contents of drawers or wardrobes thrown about, the source of most poltergeist activity can often be traced to some form of emotional disturbance in an individual within the afflicted household.

The real question, then, is whether the rite of exorcism is appropriate for the *person* involved – regardless of the individual's religious commitment. Even for atheists, the rite may be comforting and

CASTING OUT THE DEVIL

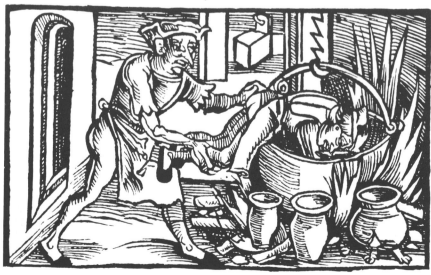

effective; while for believers, who have unwittingly engaged fanatics or incompetents to perform the rite, the results can be as terrifying as the work of the 'demon itself'.

What most victims require above all are sympathy, concern and a willingness on the part of investigators to become involved with the problem. It is very common for those affected to wonder if they are going mad; and so a warm and sympathetic investigator, who is prepared to accept the possibility that incidents of poltergeist activity are perfectly authentic, can do a tremendous amount to alleviate the acute mental distress that is often provoked in the affected individual.

Despite increasing knowledge and awareness of the diverse causes of apparently inexplicable phenomena, however, some advisers and doctors still feel unable to deal with those who fall victim and refer them instead to religious exorcists.

PERSPECTIVES

THE GHOST TRAPS OF TIBET

The most elaborate ceremonies of the Tibetan Buddhist calendar last for days or even weeks, and always incorporate a rite of exorcism, performed by the most distinguished Grand Lama of the region. When Buddhism first reached Tibet, it absorbed the ancient magical practices known as *Bön*, which flourished among the people of that remote country. One of the essential talents of a *Bön* priest was the power to expel demons and malevolent spirits from afflicted people or ill-omened places. Reflecting past traditions, it is still usual to find minor exorcists attached to a monastery, although they are not monks themselves. The *lha-ka* (mouth of the gods), whose role it is to expel the demons, is often a woman. But whether the ritual is performed by a local witch or the Grand High Lama, the essential features of the ritual are the same. The exorcist uses his or her energies to summon up powerful supernatural spirits through incantations, charms and magical recipes. The demons are summoned, threatened, and driven into a ghost-trap. They are then destroyed, usually by burning, or kept imprisoned in a suitably secure place.

The ghost traps themselves are made of wires which are meshed into patterns. An essential part of the exorcism ritual is the linking of this apparatus to participants by means of multi-coloured thread in order to conduct the psychic forces. Researchers have even questioned whether the *Bön* magicians of ancient times were perhaps conversant with some 'forgotten' aspect of astral physics

Exorcism itself can take many forms. If the main object of intervention by a clergyman is to relieve an undefined 'feeling', this can often be achieved through a religious service or blessing, or by encouraging the victim to accept that the 'atmosphere' of the affected room or house in not malign. It may take a while to convince the victim; but if the exorcist is caring and patient, this approach can often eliminate symptoms.

A full exorcism cannot be authorised, however, until a thorough examination of the circumstances of the victim has been undertaken. Normally, this process involves obtaining a report from the family doctor, an assessment from the local clergyman and, often, the views of a social worker. Indicating the more balanced approach now being adopted by some responsible member of the Churches, one bishop has said that he would not consider giving his approval to an exorcism unless a medical expert were present, or had at least examined the victim and had agreed that such a service might assist. And it should be stressed that a theatrical performance, complete with bell, book and candle, is usually considered inappropriate nowadays.

Many victims of poltergeist activity obtain relief as a result of the introduction of a religious ceremony into their households, though it is by no means certain that the effects of such ceremonies are lasting. Unfortunately, just as many people endure even greater suffering in the wake of a request for an exorcism; and there is still a body of fanatics, both clerics and laymen, who have little or no knowledge of psychology or parapsychology and whose ridiculous and scaremongering activity serve merely to increase the distress of those whom they claim to be able to help.

In Hastings, Sussex, in 1979, for example, a canon so harassed a disturbed victim, who was

On the island of Réunion in the Indian Ocean, Firmin V., right, a Creole plantation worker, reacts violently as exorcist Madame Visnelda summons an evil spirit from his body.
After an equally violent spiritual struggle, the Italian woman, above, lies peacefully at the end of a ceremony of exorcism.
Medieval thinkers regarded the poltergeist as a physical manifestation of the devil. In the woodcut, left, 'The Poltergeist in the Kitchen', a cook is being pushed face-first by a poltergeist into his cauldron of boiling water.

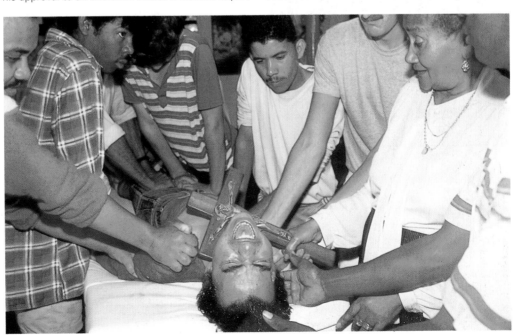

suffering from the effects of the menopause and a drug problem, that she had to be admitted to a clinic for three months' treatment. The woman's condition could well have become far more serious if her husband had not stopped the canon in the middle of his 'treatment' and told him to leave. In 1977, a family in the Midlands was also subjected to a horrifying sequence of 'cures'. First, their house was blessed by an archbishop and a local vicar. Then, a religious group visited the victimised family (who were suffering from mass hallucinations) and held a two-hour 'stomping session'. Within a few months, two seances had been held in the house, and numerous 'spiritualist' mediums had called upon the family, each providing a different (and usually nonsensical) explanation for the imagined phenomena. One claimed that the house was haunted by the evil spirit of a tall negro; another informed the family that the incidents were to be attributed to the influence of a ginger-haired dwarf. The family was able to return to normal only after a parapsychologist had spent a few hours with the mentally disturbed wife, making arrangements for a local doctor to visit.

'I was told to bury a snail underneath an oak tree at midnight, then to walk around the tree reciting the Lord's Prayer three times,' one victim of poltergeist activity told an investigator. This remarkable piece of advice was offered to her not in 1777, as one might have imagined, but two centuries later. The woman sought treatment for a psychological ailment, and the phenomena that had been distressing her promptly ceased.

But psychological treatment is not always the correct method for dealing with such incidents. Often a simpler 'cure' will help. A woman in Hampshire, who claimed that she was 'anti-religious', was disturbed enough by a minor outbreak of inexplicable incidents to consider calling upon the

*In*Focus

THE SOLEMN RITE

During an exorcism in the Italian church of St Vicinius, in Sarsina, below, the iron ring – a relic of the saint, who wore it about his neck, with heavy weights attached – serves as a penance.

Some people may view with grave misgivings the activities of certain 'professional' exorcists. In recent years, newspapers have reported a growing number of cases in which unfortunate victims have suffered severe mental (and, indeed, physical) distress; and several people have been found guilty of manslaughter and

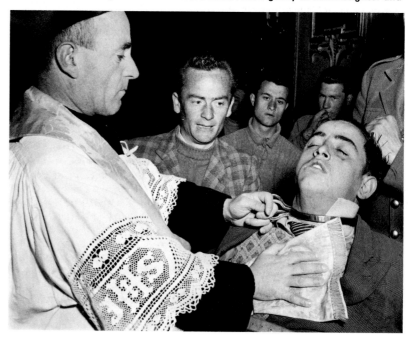

services of her local vicar. Initially, however, she confided in her mother-in-law, a spiritualist, who recommended that she should attend a 'rescue seance' to try to remove the 'troubled spirit'. (This procedure has occasionally been known to help, though it is potentially dangerous if conducted by people without adequate experience.)

// AN EXORCISM, IN FACT,

IS NO MORE THAN SURRENDERING

TO GOD AND SAYING 'PLEASE LORD,

CLEAN UP THE MESS'. //

DOM ROBERT PETITPIERRE

The suggestion made the victim somewhat apprehensive; so instead she took her problem to a parapsychologist. On his advice, she used a 'magic sign' to enable her to cope with the disturbance, and in two weeks the household had returned to normal. Needless to say, there was nothing 'magic' about the sign that she used: it was simply a device, an aid – and a successful one.

The English medium Donald Page, left, is seen, carrying out an 'exorcism' on a woman patient. Whatever explanations may be put forward for the ritual and its outcome, there is little doubt that a considerable amount of physical energy is expended by the medium.

committed to prison as a result of ignorant attempts at something of which they had no understanding or experience. Even within the ranks of the Anglican and Roman Catholic churches, there is some disquiet concerning the principles and practices that are involved.

In both churches, the ritual of exorcism is based upon the belief that a person or a place may be 'possessed' by an evil spirit or spirits, and that the appropriate words and ceremonies can be used to 'command' the evil spirit to leave. The form of the ritual is very simple, and it appears that the most important element is the strength of personality of the exorcist himself.

Since about AD 250, a ceremony of exorcism has been a part of the baptismal service in the Roman Catholic church. This does not mean that candidates are considered to be 'possessed'; rather, it is regarded rather as a ceremony to remove the effects of original sin.

The exorcism of those considered to be possessed by evil spirits is rigorously controlled in Roman Catholic canon law, and was established in the *Rituale of Pope Urban VIII*. A similar ceremony of exorcism has been retained within the canon of the Anglican church, but it is seldom performed in its original form.

In the earliest days of Christianity, exorcism was a ceremony that could be practised by anybody. Any major exorcism now requires the authorisation of a bishop before it may be performed, but many parish priests (and also certain specialist

practitioners, recognised within the body of the church) have been known to carry out private exorcisms.

The form of words in the ritual varies considerably. One practitioner, for instance, begins with the traditional words: 'I rebuke thee! I abjure thee and summon thee forth from this man...' On the other hand, Dom Robert Petitpierre, an Anglican monk and Church of England authority on all psychic matters, has written of the ritual: 'An exorcism, in fact, is no more than surrendering to God and saying "Please Lord, clean up the mess".'

The Rev. Neil-Smith, of Hampstead, London, above, has been one of the most active of Anglican exorcists. At one time, he claimed to have performed over 2,000 exorcisms within a period of four years.

One young man in Richmond, Surrey, accidentally discovered his own method of disposing of an 'evil spirit', which offered – not to him, perhaps, but to a scientific observer – evidence that the phenomena he was experiencing were basically psychological in nature. After three months of suffering from 'cracking and popping noises and strange lights on the landing', he was determined to confront and eliminate the poltergeist. One morning, exhausted and irritated, he swore at the 'thing'. From then on, he experienced no further incidents. In some cases, a symbol may certainly help; and distress may be reduced to an acceptable level, depending on the state of the victim and confidence in the 'power' or 'force' of the symbol.

Yet although the number of cases of poltergeist activity reported appears to be increasing – and there are many possible reasons for this, including the stresses of modern life, and a greater willingness among victims to admit to experiences – the success rate of exorcism is apparently declining. Indeed, a mere 20 per cent of exorcisms are now considered successful, and then only after repeated visits by authorised exorcists. As the waning of religious belief gradually makes way for the scientific study of phenomena hitherto regarded as supernatural, the days of the exorcist may be numbered.

The New Testament tells how Christ himself expelled demons by a 'word of power'. The act was also said to be a sign of the coming of God's Kingdom. Evil spirits were believed to issue from the body's orifices. The decorated initial, right, from a 12th-century manuscript in Winchester Cathedral library, shows a 'little blue devil' emerging from the mouth of a possessed man.

SEX, SORCERY AND SEANCES

MANY VICTORIANS REGARDED SEANCES – USUALLY HELD IN DARKENED ROOMS – AS A CLOAK FOR SCANDALOUS IMPROPRIETY. FOR SOME OCCULTISTS, HOWEVER, THERE SEEMS TO HAVE BEEN A LINK BETWEEN SEX AND PSI

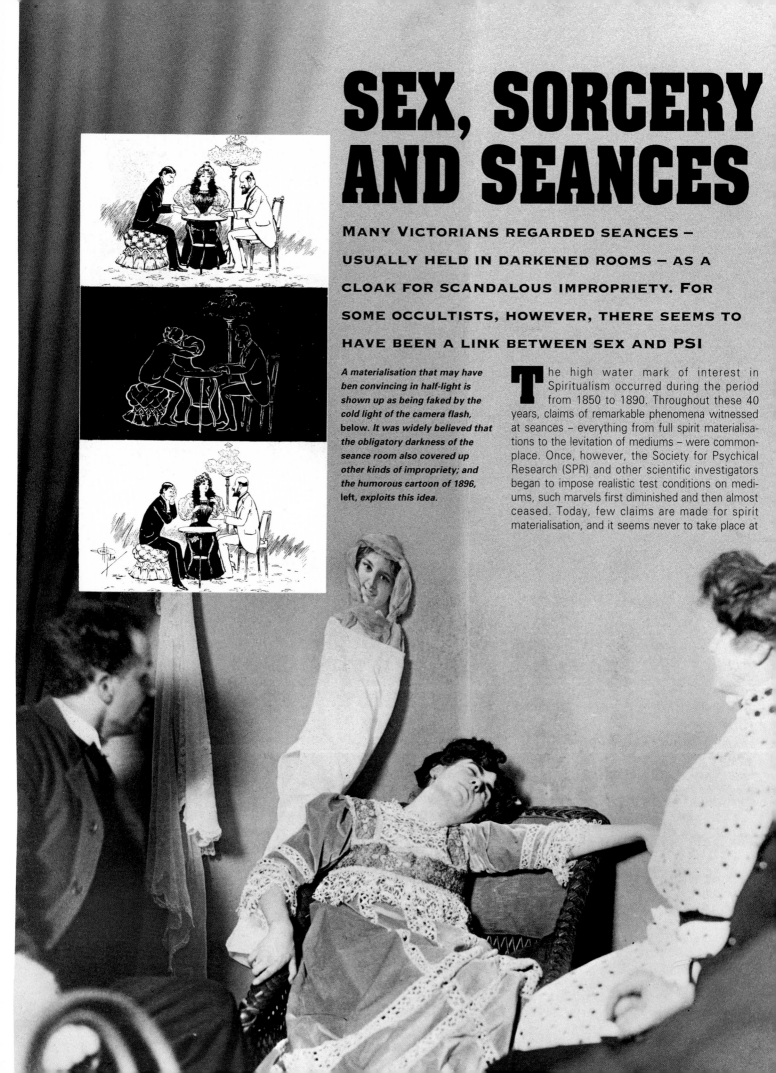

A materialisation that may have ben convincing in half-light is shown up as being faked by the cold light of the camera flash, below. It was widely believed that the obligatory darkness of the seance room also covered up other kinds of impropriety; and the humorous cartoon of 1896, left, exploits this idea.

The high water mark of interest in Spiritualism occurred during the period from 1850 to 1890. Throughout these 40 years, claims of remarkable phenomena witnessed at seances – everything from full spirit materialisations to the levitation of mediums – were commonplace. Once, however, the Society for Psychical Research (SPR) and other scientific investigators began to impose realistic test conditions on mediums, such marvels first diminished and then almost ceased. Today, few claims are made for spirit materialisation, and it seems never to take place at

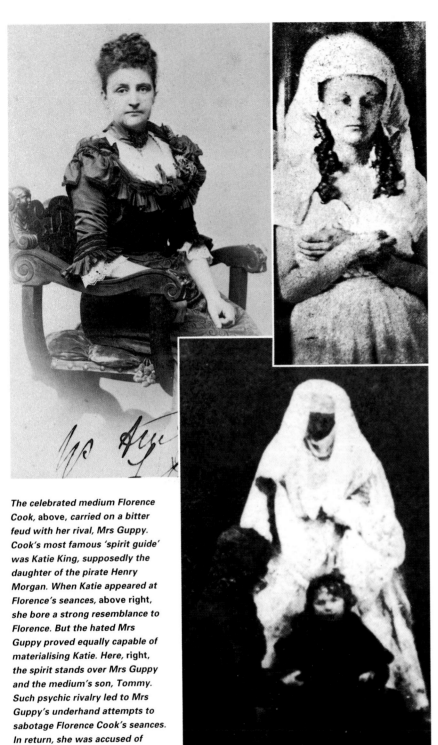

The celebrated medium Florence Cook, above, carried on a bitter feud with her rival, Mrs Guppy. Cook's most famous 'spirit guide' was Katie King, supposedly the daughter of the pirate Henry Morgan. When Katie appeared at Florence's seances, above right, she bore a strong resemblance to Florence. But the hated Mrs Guppy proved equally capable of materialising Katie. Here, right, the spirit stands over Mrs Guppy and the medium's son, Tommy. Such psychic rivalry led to Mrs Guppy's underhand attempts to sabotage Florence Cook's seances. In return, she was accused of running a house of assignation.

" MRS GUPPY USED HER PRETENDED MEDIUMSHIP FOR BASE PURPOSES, AND GAVE SEANCES SOLELY... TO ENABLE CERTAIN DISREPUTABLE PARTIES TO FURTHER CARRY OUT THEIR LEWD PROPENSITIES. "

all in the presence of non-believers and under rigid test conditions.

There is, in fact, strong reason to believe that every professional Victorian medium, with the possible exception of D.D. Home, practised fraud at one time or another. Even those who may have possessed genuine paranormal powers were not averse to practising deception when 'the power was weak' or 'the guide could not be reached'. So it is perhaps not surprising that men and women who were prepared to produce fake spirit phenomena in order to extract money from the pockets of the bereaved were also prepared discreetly to defy Victorian morality. Some female mediums became notorious for this, and even Spiritualist newspapers made veiled references to 'moral degeneration' as an occupational disease of mediumship, usually attributing it to possession by evil spirits. A more likely explanation, however, is that some mediums simply did not care about Victorian society's attitude towards sex.

Allowance must also be made for the normally sternly repressed sexual emotions, fantasies and memories, which were likely to erupt when any respectable Victorian entered a trance. In 1888, for example, one anonymous member of the SPR reported that he or she had seen: 'a medium, at others times calm and respectable, suddenly under some mysterious influence or control, break out into a tirade of the most horrible blasphemous and obscene language.'

Curiously enough, the writer of the above report fell victim to the same kind of phenomenon when experimenting with automatic writing: 'At last... the pencil settled down to steady writing, and there came the most filthy, vile language such as the mind could never have imagined.'

A CLOAK FOR PROSTITUTION?

Spiritualism seems even to have served as a cloak for prostitution and similar activities. Indeed, a feud between two mediums, Florence Cook and Mrs Guppy, involved some curious allegations concerning the latter. Mrs Guppy was a powerful physical medium whose accomplishments had included the materialisation at seances of such diverse objects as fresh flowers and a large block of ice. But in January 1873, she found that her clients were being drawn away by what she referred to as the 'doll face' of Florence Cook, who was young and attractive. It is of interest that Mrs Guppy should consider Florence's appearance, rather than her psychic abilities, to be the reason for increasing popularity.

Mrs Guppy, therefore, decided to take drastic measures. In the guise of enquirers, a certain James Clark and two other friends of Mrs Guppy were to attend one of Florence Cook's seances. When a 'spirit' – whom they suspected to be Florence Cook in disguise – manifested itself, they were to throw oil of vitriol (concentrated sulphuric acid) in its face.

Mrs Guppy also tried to enlist the help of two American mediums, Mr and Mrs Holmes, in her scheme, but they indignantly refused and sent a warning to the intended victim. In revenge, Mrs Guppy regularly sent roughs to break up the Holmes' seances. Such activity ceased only when, in a letter to the London Dialectical Society, Holmes threatened to expose her: 'If necessary, I can give you the details of the infamous transactions of Mrs Guppy with Miss Emily Berry, 1 Hyde Park Place, also why Mrs Guppy used her pretended mediumship for base purposes, and gave seances solely for assignation to better enable certain disreputable parties to further carry out their lewd propensities.'

In the 19th century, so-called 'black' magicians were usually those occultists who employed sex in the attempt to unlock those gates that lead to the paranormal. There were a surprising number of such practitioners. Of course, they took care to avoid adverse publicity and tended to speak and write of their activities in coyly symbolic language. One was P.B. Randolph, an American who called himself a Rosicrucian. He believed that, in the course of human copulation, both men and women produce 'psychic secretions', as well as the more familiar male semen and female lubricants. These positive and negative psychic secretions, said Randolph, are 'thesis and antithesis', and combine into a 'new and higher unity' that sets in flow a current of psychic force. If certain secret techniques are used for directing this current into the proper channels, both participants in the sexual act will receive physical, mental and spiritual benefits.

In typically vague and flowery language, Randolph described how he had acquired this knowledge: 'I made love to, and was loved by, a dusky maiden . . . I . . . learned the fundamental principle of the White Magic of Love; subsequently I became acquainted with some dervishes . . . and of these devout practices of a simple but sublime and holy magic . . . I obtained . . . the ELIXIR OF LIFE . . . the water of beauty and perpetual youth, and the philosopher's stone.'

Another 19th-century practitioner of sexual occultism was Thomas Lake Harris – English by birth but American by naturalisation. His method involved something he called 'archnatural respiration' – probably nothing more than deliberate hyperventilation of the lungs. But he also dabbled in an occult sexual technique – *sympneumata* – that involved a couple breathing in unison while they made love.

ASTRAL EROTICISM

An adaptation of *sympneumata* has also been employed by black magicians of the present century for purposes of sexual seduction. The would-be lover sits as near as possible to his intended victim, who is totally unaware of his intentions at first. He gauges her breathing by the rise and fall of her breasts and, once he has established the exact rhythm, begins to breathe in precise unison with her. The sorcerer continues this for a period of between three and five minutes, and then contracts the muscles of his anus for five to ten seconds. This, supposedly, establishes an 'astral link' between the two people involved, by bringing into action the man's *muladhara chakra*, a centre of psychic activity that, according to some occultists, controls the libido. It is situated, they claim, in a part of the 'subtle body' corresponding to the area between the anus and the genitals.

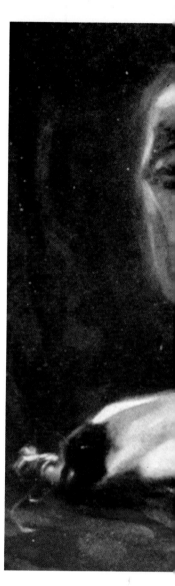

// THE POWER OF THE ORGASM AND THE MAGIC STUFF THAT COMES WITH IT WILL SUFFUSE THE ROOM OR TEMPLE AND THE WORSHIPPER IS INFLAMED WITH BLISS. //

PETER REDGROVE, THE BLACK GODDESS AND THE SIXTH SENSE

THE FAMOUS FLYING GUPPY

During the late Victorian era, Mrs Samuel Guppy was one of London's most prominent mediums. Born Agnes Nichols, her mediumistic powers were first discovered in 1866 – the year before she married Samuel Guppy – by the great British naturalist Alfred Russel Wallace during investigations into Spiritualism. He found young Agnes at his sister's house where she was conducting seances that included raps, table movements, levitation and apports. So renowned did Mrs Guppy become that her seances were even attended by minor European royalty, such as Princess Marguerite of Naples (who asked for, and received, cacti, which dropped from the air on to the seance table). Other apports included stinging nettles, lobsters, live eels and butterflies.

In spite of her success, however, Mrs Guppy was known to be highly jealous of another London medium, Florence Cook. Some said this was because Miss Cook was more attractive. Whatever the case, rumour also implicated Mrs Guppy in a potential scandal when an American medium claimed that Mrs Guppy's seances were, in fact, a hotbed of sexual intrigue.

The most famous incident in Mrs Guppy's career occurred on 3 June 1871 when she was, apparently, transported – within three minutes – from her home in Highbury, North London, to the house of another medium, Charles Williams, at 61 Lamb's Conduit Street, some three miles away. Williams was holding a seance, when a sitter jokingly asked the spirit control, Katie King, to bring Mrs Guppy. She arrived at the seance – out of nowhere, crash-landing on the table – in a loose dressing gown and wearing a pair of bedroom slippers. She seemed to be in a trance, and had one arm over her eyes. Before long, her boots, hat and clothes also miraculously travelled from her home.

The magician then gradually increases his rate of breathing until it reaches the rate characteristic of the height of sexual activity. The 'astral link' ensures that the emotions normally associated with this rapid breathing are communicated to the woman, and she immediately experiences arousal.

Some of those who practise *sympneumata* attempt to establish 'astral links' with their victims for more than mere sexual satisfaction. Indeed, once the established link has been sufficiently strengthened, the bedmate can be transformed into a disciple. Thus, it is claimed, one more black magician comes into existence.

All this is very reminiscent of an ancient idea about vampirism – that victims themselves in turn become vampires, seeking out the living for nourishment. Many occultists have been well aware of such similarities and have theorised elaborately on the subject of 'psychic vampirism', by means of which psychosexual energy is drained from the victim. This can be done in several ways: some vampires are supposed to be sufficiently powerful to absorb energy simply by sitting in the same room as the objects of attack, while others have to engage in 'astral projection' and, in ghostly form, visit their victims as they sleep. Still others can extract energy from a partner only via sexual activity. Really expert vampires, one group asserts, can sexually exhaust their victims to the point of death. In this way, the vampire not only obtains the physical strength of the victim but acquires his or her soul as a familiar spirit.

THE MASTER SATURNUS

An offshoot of the group that produced this occult teaching was 'Saturn-Gnosis', active in Germany from the 1920s until its suppression by the Nazis. It was later revived, around 1950, by a man who called himself the 'Master Saturnus'.

The leaders of Saturn-Gnosis taught an extraordinarily complex system of sex magic, either based on their own imagination and fancy or on some secret tradition. Indeed, the system is so involved that it seems hardly worth the trouble of following it, however beneficial the supposed results. For example, before engaging in sexual activity, initiates of the group were instructed to consult ephemerides (tables giving the daily positions of the Sun, Moon and planets in relation to the zodiac). If Venus and Mars were square – at an angle of 90° to one another, as seen from the Earth – copulation should be carried out in a sitting position. The exact nature of the sitting position would also have to be decided in accordance with astrological conditions: thus if Venus were in a 'stronger' zodiacal position than Mars, the woman would sit on the man's lap. When the couple eventually decided on their appropriate posture, they were not to start their activities before burning incense and placing defensive occult symbols around themselves.

The type of sex magic associated with Saturn-Gnosis and similar European groups spread across the Atlantic in the 1920s and has continued to flourish ever since. For example, the Great Brotherhood of God was led by a one-time resident of the Abbey of Thelema. It was extremely active in the 1930s and attracted a surprisingly large membership. Louis Culling even published a detailed account of his progress in this society. He had to pass numerous tests, during one of which he was required to engage in continuous sexual intercourse, without ejaculation, for a period of three hours. Culling not only passed all his tests, rising to high office in the brotherhood, but carried out much research in the field of occult sexuality. His major triumph was his discovery that *damiana*, a Mexican herb traditionally reputed to possess stimulant qualities, was a 'psychic aphrodisiac'. Those taking it, he claimed, benefited not only physically, by becoming more potent, but also astrally: apparently, they became so filled with psychosexual energy that they were irresistible to members of the opposite sex.

If Culling's published account is to be believed, a series of experiments he carried out in 1962 proved the paranormal effects of *damiana* beyond all reasonable doubt. The 69-year-old researcher began to drink a daily cupful of an infusion of the wondrous herb. After only 10 days, women over 30 years younger than himself began to take an interest in him. Four days later, his libido bursting with the energy of a man half-a-century younger, he left his Los Angeles home for a short holiday in the Mexican border town of Tijuana.

With no trouble at all, he got into conversation with a young waitress, who agreed to visit him at his hotel. Fortified by *damiana*, the couple engaged in extended and ecstatic copulation. The waitress is said to have been delighted by her experience.

Such, then, are the claims of the sexual occultists. They range from the absurd to the plausible, and suggest a two-way traffic between the psychosexual energy of the libido and the outer world: the libido, it is said, can move matter, as in poltergeist phenomena; and it can itself be revitalised and manipulated by drugs, by rituals, or by feats of psychic exertion. Diverse as these beliefs are, they are alike in the stress placed on a 20th-century obsession – the central importance of sex.

The erotic element in the conventional vampire tale is made explicit in the painting, above, which comes from a Viennese postcard of 1900. Some forms of sex magic are said to be akin to vampirism, the victim becoming a disciple of the magician.

Louis Culling, right, gained high office in a brotherhood of sex magicians.

THE ELIXIR OF LIFE

THE TWIN AIMS OF ALCHEMY WERE DISCOVERY OF THE PHILOSOPHER'S STONE, WHICH HAD THE PURPOSE OF TURNING BASE METALS INTO GOLD, AND AN ELIXIR THAT WOULD CONFER ETERNAL LIFE. THIS QUEST ATTRACTED TWO OF THE STRANGEST IMAGINABLE FIGURES IN THIS REALM OF MAGICAL CHEMISTRY WHOSE RESULTS ARE SAID TO HAVE BEEN SPECTACULAR

Alchemists grew old and decrepit in their quest for the Elixir of Life, as shown in the painting above. Yet stories persist that some fortunate practitioners did indeed discover ways to survive beyond their natural span.

Theophrastus Bombastus von Hohenheim, below, city physician of Basel, contributed much to alchemical theory, as well as to more orthodox pharmacy.

'Always drunk and always lucid,' was how a biographer described Theophrastus Bombastus von Hohenheim (c.1493-1541), who dubbed himself 'Paracelsus' (meaning 'like Celsus', the ancient Roman physician). His extraordinary career included the study of magic under Hans von Trittenheim at Würzburg in Germany, working for a year in the silver mines and metallurigical workshops of Sigismund Fugge in the Tyrol, travelling through Germany, Italy, France, the Netherlands, England, Scandinavia and Russia, serving as an army surgeon in Italy, and taking a medical degree at the University of Ferrara, Italy. Subsequently, in 1526, Paracelsus was appointed city physician of Basel, Switzerland, and celebrated this with a remarkable tirade in the city square. Into a brass pan full of glowing coals, he thrust the works of Avicenna, the 11th-century Arab philosopher, and of Galen, the second-century Greek medical authority. He then sprinkled sulphur and saltpetre over them so that they were consumed in spectacular flames, and declared loudly:

'If your physicians only knew that their prince Galen – they call none like him – was sticking in Hell, from whence he has sent letters to me, they would make the sign of the cross upon themselves with a fox's tail. In the same way, your Avicenna sits in the vestibule of the Infernal portal; and I have disputed with him about his . . . Tincture of the Philosophers, his Quintessence, and Philosopher's Stone... and all the rest. O you hypocrites, who despise the truths taught you by a great physician [he meant himself]... Come then, and listen, impostors who prevail only by the authority of your high positions! After my death, my disciples will burst forth and drag you to the light, and shall expose your dirty drugs, wherewith up to this time you have compassed the death of princes... '

In spite of such an egotistical style, Paracelsus was an important influence in the development of the science of pharmacy, being among the first to recognise that the processes of alchemy were basically the same as those of cooking – he even dignified the man who lit and tended the fires with the title of 'alchemist'. And he replaced the four elements of Aristotle (earth, water, air and fire), with three 'hypostatical principles' – mercury, sulphur and salt. The term 'hypostatical' meant that these were not the ordinary substances known by these names: they were, rather, three ideal substances, which a 17th-century text described in these terms:

'Mercury is that sharp, permeating, ethereal and very pure fluid to which all nutrition, sense, motion, power, colours and retardation of age are due. It is derived from air and water; it is the food of life...

'Sulphur is that sweet, oleaginous and viscid [glutinous] balsam conserving the natural heat of the parts, instrument of all vegetation [unconscious activity of plants or animals, such as assimilating food], increase and transmutation, and the fountain and origin of all colours. It is inflammable, yet has great power of conglutinating [sticking together] extreme contraries.

'Salt is that dry saline body preserving mixtures from putrefaction, having wonderful powers of dissolving, coagulating, cleansing, evacuating, conferring solidity, consistency, taste and the like. It

Two targets of the wrath of Paracelsus were the Greek writer Galen, above, an authority on drugs, and the Arab ibn Sina, known in Europe as Avicenna, below, author of The Canon of Medicine.

resembles earth, not as being cold and dry, but as being firm and fixed.'

Paracelsus saw these three principles in terms of spirit (mercury), soul (sulphur) and body (salt). As he himself put it in one of his alchemical writings:

'But as there are many kinds of fruit, so there are many kinds of sulphur, salt and mercury. A different sulphur is in gold, another in silver, another in lead, another in iron, tin, etc. Also a different one in sapphire, another in the emerald, another in the ruby, chrysolite, amethyst, magnets, etc. Also another in stones, flint, salts, springwaters, etc... '

This kind of thinking led Paracelsus to the search for the quintessence of each material, the refined and purified extract that was the essential part of it. Supposedly, he identified this with the mercury specific to that substance. Indeed, in his public speech in Basel, he was, in fact, contrasting the quintessences of various metals, which he prepared by distillation, to common 'dirty drugs'.

INNOVATIVE ALCHEMY

The concept of hypostatic mercury, sulphur and salt gave a new impetus to alchemical enquiry; and Paracelsus achieved apparent success in medical treatment with some of his quintessences. They were probably weak acid solutions, pepped up in some instances with alcohol.

The ideas of Paracelsus also encouraged the search for the Elixir of Life. This remarkable substance supposedly conferred longevity. The search for immortality had long interested Chinese alchemists, for instance, who advocated taking special medicines, often of mineral content. In Europe, too, alchemists were rumoured at various times to have gained immortality. One was Nicolas Flamel, a thrifty and industrious scrivener (scribe and copyist) in 14th-century Paris. In 1357, he bought a very old and large illuminated book.

For 21 years, Flamel tried without success to find someone who could explain these pictures to him. At last, his wife Perenelle suggested that he should travel to Spain to seek out some learned Jew who could shed light on the matter. Flamel decided to make the famous pilgrimage to the shrine of St James at Compostela; and so, with his pilgrim's staff and broad-brimmed hat, and carrying carefully made copies of the mysterious illustrations, he set out on foot.

SECRET PROCESSES

Once he had made his devotions at the shrine, he travelled on to the city of León, in northern Spain, where by chance he made the acquaintance of a certain Master Canches, a learned Jewish physician. When Canches saw the pictures, he was 'ravished with great astonishment and joy', recognising them as parts of a book that he had long believed lost. He made up his mind at once to return with Flamel to France. But at Orléans, wearied and old, he died. Flamel, having seen him buried, returned alone to Paris.

'I had now the *prima materia,* the first principles, yet not their first preparation, which is a thing most difficult, above all things in the world... Finally, I found that which I desired, which I also knew by the strong scent and odour thereof. Having this, I easily accomplished the Mastery... The first time that I made projection [accomplished transmutation] was upon Mercury, whereof I turned half a pound [227 grammes], or thereabouts, into pure silver, better than that of the Mine, as I myself assayed [tested], and made others assay many times. This was upon a Monday, the 17th of January about

Two pages from an early copy of **The Book of Abraham the Jew** *are shown left and above left. The lower picture shows those who seek for gold in the garden. The figure at bottom right, is said to be Nicolas Flamel himself. In the upper picture, the rider mounted on a black lion represents gold in maceration; the second figure, on a red lion, represents the inner ferment; and the crowned rider on a white lion symbolises success.*

'The cover of it was of brass, well bound, all engraven with letters or strange figures... This I know that I could not read them nor were they either Latin or French letters... As to the matter that was written within, it was engraved (as I suppose) with an iron pencil or graver upon . . . bark leaves, and curiously coloured... '

On the first page was written in golden letters: 'Abraham the Jew, Priest, Prince, Levite, Astrologer and Philosopher, to the Nation of the Jews dispersed by the Wrath of God in France, wisheth Health'. Flamel subsequently referred to this manuscript as *The Book of Abraham the Jew.* The dedication was followed by execrations against anyone who was neither priest nor scribe and who might read the book. As Flamel was a scribe, he was emboldened to read further.

The author intended to give the dispersed Jewish people assistance in paying their taxes to the Roman authorities by teaching them how to transmute base metals into gold. The instructions were clear and easy to follow; but unfortunately they referred only to the later stages of the process. The only guidance to the important earlier stages was said to be in the illustrations given on the fourth and fifth leaves of the book. To his great disappointment, Flamel found that, although these pictures were well painted:

'Yet by that could no man ever have been able to understand it without being well skilled in their Qabalah, which is a series of old traditions, and also to have been well studied in their books.'

Nicolas Flamel, left – *depicted in an early 19th-century portrait – is said to have succeeded in transmuting mercury into gold.*

In a further picture from The Book of Abraham the Jew, *right*, *the red and white flowers stand for stages in the 'Great Work', the dragons for sophic (that is, 'ideal') mercury, and the griffins for a combination of the lion (the fixed principle) and the eagle (the volatile principle).*

The 18th-century engraving, above, is of the frescoes painted for Flamel in the churchyard of the Holy Innocents in Paris, and which survived for 400 years. A pair of small figures below the centre represents Flamel and his wife Perenelle, while the panels at the top show seven of the illustrations from The Book of Abraham the Jew.

noon, in my home, Perenelle only being present, in the year of the restoring of mankind 1382.'

Three months later, Flamel made his first transmutation into gold. He and Perenelle put their new-found wealth to good use. They endowed:

'Fourteen hospitals, three chapels and seven churches, in the city of Paris, all which we had new built from the ground, and enriched with great gifts and revenues, with many reparations in their churchyards. We also have done at Boulogne about as much as we have done at Paris, not to speak of the charitable acts which we both did to particular poor people, principally to widows and orphans... '

After Flamel's death in 1419, rumours began to circulate. Hoping that the Philosopher's Stone might still be hidden in one of his houses, people searched through them again and again, until one was reduced to a pile of rubble. There were stories that both Perenelle and Nicolas were still alive; that she had gone to live in Switzerland while he had buried a log in her grave; and that, later, he did the same at his own 'funeral'.

In the centuries since, legends have persisted that the wealthy alchemist managed to defeat death. The 17th-century traveller Paul Lucas, while in Asia Minor, met a distinguished Turkish philosopher. He was told that true philosophers had known the secret of prolonging life for anything up to a thousand years. 'At last I took the liberty of naming the celebrated Flamel who, it was said, possessed the Philosopher's Stone, yet was certainly dead. He smiled at my simplicity, and asked with an air of mirth: "Do you really believe this? No, no, my friend, Flamel is still living; neither he nor his wife has yet tasted death. It is not above three years since I left both... in India; he is one of my best friends".'

CHEATING DEATH

In 1761, Flamel and his wife were said to have attended the opera in Paris. Later, there were other sightings too. So what are we to make, for instance, of an account in *Le Corbeau Menteur* (The Lying Raven) by the 19th-century writer Ninian Bres?

'He was a little less than middle height, stooping somewhat with the weight of years, but still with a firm step and a clear eye, and with a complexion strangely smooth and transparent, like fine alabaster. Both he and the woman with him – clearly his wife, although she appeared almost imperceptibly the older and more decisive of the two – were dressed in a style that seemed only a few years out of fashion and yet had an indefinable air of antiquity about it. I stood, half-concealed in a little archway toward the end of the Boulevard du Temple: my hands were stained with acid, and my topcoat stank of the furnace. As the couple came abreast of the spot where I stood, Flamel turned toward me and seemed about to speak, but Perenelle drew him quickly on, and they were almost at once lost in the crowd.

'You ask how I am so confident that this was Nicolas Flamel? I tell you that I have spent many hours in the Bibliothèque Nationale, poring over *The Book of Abraham the Jew*: look carefully at the first side of the fifth leaf and there, in the lower right-hand corner of the representation of those who seek for gold in the garden, you will see the face that searched mine that evening on the Boulevard du Temple, and that has haunted my dreams ever since.'

❝ A KEY FEATURE OF PARACELSIAN ALCHEMY AND MEDICINE WAS THE IMPORTANCE OF CELESTIAL ENERGIES AND INFLUENCES... EACH METAL WAS RELATED TO A SPECIFIC PLANET AND WAS SAID TO CONTAIN WITHIN ITSELF AN ARCANUM, A CELESTIAL POWER DERIVED DIRECTLY FROM ITS RULING PLANET... CARRYING OUT SUCH ALCHEMICAL WORK, PARACELSUS MAINTAINED, WAS LIKE RECREATING THE UNIVERSE IN MINIATURE. ❞

CHERRY GILCHRIST,

ALCHEMY, THE GREAT WORK

HITLER AND THE HOLY LANCE

THE LANCE THAT PIERCED CHRIST'S SIDE AT HIS CRUCIFIXION BECAME A HOLY TALISMAN FOR THE TEUTONIC WARLORDS OF EUROPE. IN THE 20TH CENTURY, IT WAS PLUNDERED BY ADOLF HITLER, WHO KNEW ITS MYSTICAL SIGNIFICANCE ALL TOO WELL, AND LINKED WITH IT HIS DESTINY

In the streets of Vienna in 1913, a down-and-out former art student tried vainly to make a living by selling postcard-sized watercolours. Occasionally, driven off the streets by cold, he would wander through the corridors of the Hofburg Museum. Here, he was particularly fascinated by a number of valuable pieces known as the Habsburg regalia. Among these, the unprepossessing young vagrant, Adolf Hitler, paid special attention to the Holy Lance – reputed to be the spear that had pierced Christ's side while on the cross.

The legend concerning the Holy Lance takes its origin from *John 19: 33-37:*

'But when they came to Jesus, and saw that he was dead already, they brake not his legs: but one of the soldiers with a spear pierced his side, and forthwith came there out blood and water. And he that saw it bare record, and his record is true: and he knoweth that he saith true, that ye might believe. For these things were done that the scripture should be fulfilled, A bone of him shall not be broken. And again another scripture saith, They shall look on him whom they pierced.'

The verse following this tells how Joseph of Arimathaea gained permission to take the body of Jesus and, helped by Nicodemus, laid it in a tomb on the night of Good Friday.

Other oral and written traditions, beginning with the earliest Christians and continuing to the Middle Ages, depict the rich Jewish philanthropist, Joseph, as obsessed with the artefacts associated with the dead Christ. He is said to have preserved the cross itself, the nails, the crown of thorns, and also the shroud from which Christ rose on the third day. Using clues left by Joseph, Helena – mother of the first Christian emperor, Constantine – was apparently able to rediscover these relics. But even before Christ's death, according to the same traditions, Joseph had begun collecting. After the Last

Supper, he took charge of the cup in which Jesus had consecrated the bread and wine; and after the resurrection, he kept it alongside the spear. Subsequently, the two items became known as the Holy Grail and the Holy Lance, respectively.

Joseph's subsequent travels with the Grail and the Lance are the subject of folk tales and legends that are to be found in almost every country in Europe. In Britain, he is said to have hidden the Grail at Glastonbury. Afterwards, we are told, he thrust his staff into the ground, where it sprouted to become the still-surviving Glastonbury Thorn, which thereafter is known mysteriously to have bloomed only at Christmas-time.

Romantic writers, beginning with the French poet Chrétien de Troyes in about 1180, took up the legend and linked the fate of the Holy Grail and the Holy Lance with the adventures of King Arthur and the Knights of the Round Table, notably with Lancelot, Gawain and Perceval.

Alongside these romantic stories – themselves based on Celtic tradition and scraps of historical fact – there ran a thread of evidence, albeit thin, that the Lance, at least, had survived the centuries, and had somehow been passed down sometimes through good hands, sometimes through unworthy ones. With its ownership, it seems, came a marked degree of power, to be used either for great good or for terrible evil.

At least four 'Holy Lances' existed in Europe during the early part of the present century. Perhaps the best-known was in the keeping of the Vatican, although the Roman Catholic Church seems to have regarded it as no more than a curio. Certainly, no preternatural powers were claimed for it by the papal authorities.

A second lance was kept in Paris, where it had been taken by St Louis in the 13th century, after his return from the Crusades in Palestine.

MIRACULOUS VISION

Another lance, preserved in Cracow, Poland, was merely a copy of the Habsburg lance. The latter probably had the best pedigree of them all. It had been discovered at Antioch, in the Near East, in 1098, during the First Crusade, but mystery – and possibly imagination – obscured the manner of its finding. Crusaders had mounted a successful siege of the city and had taken control, when a more heavily armed band of Saracens turned the tables, shutting up the Crusaders within the walls. After three weeks, water and food were running low and surrender seemed the only course. Then a priest claimed to have had a miraculous vision of the Holy Lance, buried in the church of St Peter. When excavations at the spot revealed the iron spearhead, the Crusaders were filled with a new zeal and rode out to rout their attackers.

Germanic tradition, somewhat at odds with these dates, claimed the Habsburg lance had in fact been carried as a talisman in the ninth century by Charlemagne through 47 victorious campaigns. It had also endowed him with clairvoyant powers. Only when he accidentally dropped it did Charlemagne die.

The lance later passed into the possession of Heinrich (Henry) the Fowler, who founded the royal house of the Saxons and drove the Poles eastwards – a foreshadowing, Hitler may have thought in later years, of his own destiny. After passing through the hands of five Saxon monarchs, it next fell into the possession of the succeeding Hohenstaufens of Swabia. One of the most outstanding of this line was Frederick Barbarossa, born in 1123. Before his death, 67 years later, Barbarossa conquered Italy and drove the Pope himself into exile. Again, Hitler may well have admired the brutal harshness, coupled with a charismatic personality, that led Barbarossa to success. Like Charlemagne, however, Barbarossa made the mistake of dropping the lance as he waded through a stream in Sicily, and he drowned within minutes.

This was the legend of the weapon, now among the Habsburg regalia, which so fascinated the young Hitler. He spent his first visit to the Holy Lance studying its every detail. It was just over a foot (30 centimetres) long, tapering to a slender, leaf-shaped point, and at some time the blade had been grooved to admit a nail – allegedly one of those used in the crucifixion. This had been bound into place with gold wire. The spear had been broken, and the two halves were joined by a sheath of silver, while two gold crosses had been inlaid into the base, near the haft.

The evidence of Hitler's personal fascination with the Habsburg lance rests on the testimony of Dr Walter Johannes Stein, a mathematician,

The blade of the Habsburg spear, far left, is reputed to be the lance that pierced Christ's side while he was on the cross. Because it was a holy relic, the iron blade has been extensively repaired with gold and silver during its long history. It is now bound together with wire and an inscribed 'sleeve'.

In a painting by Rubens, left, a Roman soldier confirms that Christ is dead by plunging a spear into him. According to tradition, it was revealed to the soldier at this moment that Christ was truly the Son of God and the spear acquired enduring magical potency.

Just one face in the crowds of Germans who exulted at the outbreak of the First World War, Adolf Hitler, right, was poverty-stricken and obscure at this stage, but dreaming already of leading the Nordic race to supremacy.

By selling watercolours like the one, below, Hitler scratched a living in Vienna in 1913.

economist and occultist who claimed to have met the future Führer just before the First World War. Stein, a native of Vienna, was born in 1891, the son of a rich barrister. He was to be a polymath and an intellectual adventurer until his death in 1957, taking a first degree in science and a doctorate in psychophysical research at the University of Vienna. He also became expert in archaeology, early Byzantine art and medieval history; and in the First World War, as an officer in the Austrian Army, he was decorated for gallantry.

In 1928, he published an eccentric pamphlet, *World History in the Light of the Holy Grail*, which was circulated in Germany, Holland and Britain. Just five years after that, Reichsführer Heinrich Himmler ordered that he be pressed into service with the Nazi 'Occult Bureau', but Stein escaped to Britain.

The Second World War found him in the guise of a British intelligence agent. After helping the British to obtain the plans for 'Operation Sealion' – Hitler's projected invasion of Britain – he acted as adviser to Winston Churchill on the German leader's occult involvements.

Stein never published his own memoirs; but before his death, he befriended a former Sandhurst commando officer, then a journalist, Trevor Ravenscroft. Using Stein's notices and conversations, Ravenscroft published a book, *Spear of Destiny*, in 1972, which first brought Hitler's fascination with the Habsburg spear to public attention.

But what hold could the Holy Lance, a Christian symbol, have had on the violently anti-Christian, ex-Roman Catholic Adolf Hitler? Already he was given to violent anti-Semitic rantings, and already he was a devout student of Friedrich Nietzsche's Anti-Christ, with its condemnation of Christianity as 'the ultimate Jewish consequence'.

Charlemagne, King of the Franks, above, became Holy Roman Emperor in AD 800. One of the legends that have grown up around him says that he owed his success in war to the Holy Lance.

The triumphal entry of Hitler into Vienna in March 1938 is shown below. One of his first acts was to order the removal to Germany of the Habsburg treasure, which included the Holy Lance.

Part of the answer lay in a medieval occult tradition regarding the history of the Holy Lance. As the *Gospel of John* describes, the Roman soldier who pierced Christ's side had unwittingly fulfilled the *Old Testament* prophecies (that Christ's bones would not be broken). Had he not done as he did, the destiny of Mankind would have been different. According to both Matthew and Mark, the true nature of Christ was revealed to the soldier, said to have been named Gaius Cassius Longinus, at that moment: 'And when the centurion, which stood over against him, saw that he so cried out, and gave up the ghost, he said, Truly this man was the Son of God.' *(Mark 15:39.)*

To the mind of the occultist, an instrument used for such momentous purpose would itself become the focus of magical power. As Richard Cavendish puts it, speaking of the Grail and the Lance in his book *King Arthur and the Grail:*

'A thing is not sacred because it is good. It is sacred because it contains mysterious and awesome power. It is as potent for good or evil as a huge charge of electricity. If it is tampered with, however compelling and understandable the motive, the consequences may be catastrophic for entirely innocent people.'

According to Stein, Hitler was fully aware of this concept as early as 1912: indeed, it was through Hitler's obsession with the legend of the Holy

Lance and its power as a 'magic wand' that the two men met. In the summer of 1912, Dr Stein purchased an edition of *Parsival*, a Grail romance by the 13th-century German poet Wolfram von Eschenbach, from an occult bookseller in Vienna. It was full of scribbled marginal commentaries, displaying a combination of occult learning and pathological racism. On the flyleaf, its previous owner had signed his name: Adolf Hitler. Through the bookseller, Stein traced Hitler and spent many hours with him, appalled but fascinated. Although it was to be years before the poverty-stricken postcard painter took his first steps on the road to power, there was already an evil charisma about the man. Through all the tortuous windings of his discourse, one obsession stood out clearly: he had a mystic destiny to fulfil and, according to Stein, the Holy Lance held the key.

Hitler described to Stein how the spear had acquired a special significance for him: 'I slowly became aware of a mighty presence around it, the same awesome presence which I had experienced inwardly on those rare occasions in my life when I had sensed that a great destiny awaited me... a window in the future was opened up to me through which I saw, in a single flash of illumination, a future event by which I knew beyond contradiction that the blood in my veins would one day become the vessel of the Folk-Spirit of my people.'

Hitler never revealed the nature of his 'vision'; but Stein believed that he had seen himself a quarter of a century later, in the Heldenplatz outside the Hofburg Museum, addressing Austrian Nazis and ordinary, bewildered Viennese. There, on 14 March 1938, the German Führer was to announce his annexation of Austria into the German Reich, and to give the order to carry the Habsburg regalia off to Nuremberg, spiritual home of the Nazi movement.

Taking possession of the treasure was a curious priority, in view of the fact that Hitler despised the house of Habsburg as traitors to the Germanic race. Nevertheless, on 13 October, the spear and the other items of the regalia were loaded on to an armoured train with an SS guard and taken across the German border. They were lodged in the hall of St Catherine's Church, where Hitler proposed to set up a Nazi war museum. Stein believed that once Hitler had the Holy Lance in his possession, his latent ambitions for world conquest began to grow and flourish.

> **❚❚**...THERE WAS ALREADY AN EVIL CHARISMA ABOUT THE MAN. THROUGH ALL THE TORTUOUS WINDINGS OF HIS DISCOURSE, ONE OBSESSION STOOD OUT CLEARLY: HE HAD A MYSTIC DESTINY TO FULFIL AND... THE HOLY LANCE HELD THE KEY.**❚❚**

The scene, **left,** *is from* **Parsifal,** **Wagner's last opera. Hitler was fascinated by the legend on which the opera is based. Here, the enchantress Kundry, redeemed from a life of evil, dies as Parsifal takes the Holy Grail from its shrine. He holds the Holy Lance, which, having been used to work evil by the black magician Klingsor, is an instrument of blessing in the hands of the virtuous Parsifal.**

The Luitpold Arena in Nuremberg, **bottom,** *scene of the Nazis' most spectacular pre-war rallies, saw an informal 'march past' by victorious US soldiers in April 1945,* **inset.** *In the ruins of the shattered city, the Holy Lance, with other war booty, was found in a bombproof vault.*

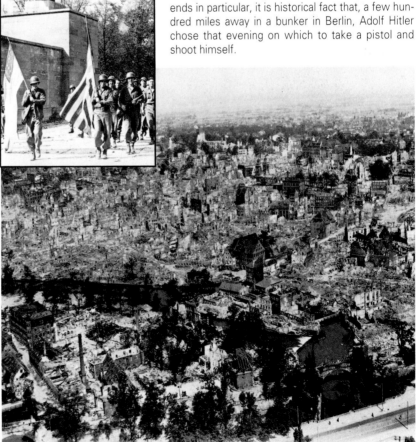

If Hitler's knowledge of the Habsburg spear's history was as extensive as Stein claimed, he must have been aware of the legends concerning the fate of Charlemagne, Barbarossa and others who had wielded it as a weapon, only to perish when it fell from their grasp. This seems to be confirmed by a chilling coincidence.

After heavy Allied bombing in October 1944, during which Nuremberg suffered extensive damage, Hitler ordered the spear, along with the rest of the Habsburg regalia, to be buried in a specially constructed vault.

Six months later, the American Seventh Army had surrounded the ancient city, which was defended by 22,000 SS troops, 100 Panzers and 22 regiments of artillery. For four days, the veteran American Thunderbird Division battered at this formidable defence until, on 20 April 1945 – Hitler's 56th birthday – the victorious Stars and Stripes was hoisted over the rubble.

During the next few days, while American troops took on the task of rounding up survivors of the Nazi military and began the long process of interrogating them, Company C of the US Army's Third Military Government Regiment, under the command of Lieutenant William Horn, were detailed to search for the Habsburg treasure. By chance, a shell had made their task easier by blowing away brickwork and revealing the entrance to the vault. After some difficulty with the vault's steel doors, Lieutenant Horn entered the underground chamber and peered through the dusty gloom. There, lying on a bed of faded red velvet, was the fabled spear of Longinus.

However sceptical critics may be about Walter Stein, the occult in general and the Holy Lance legends in particular, it is historical fact that, a few hundred miles away in a bunker in Berlin, Adolf Hitler chose that evening on which to take a pistol and shoot himself.

was terrified. I could see it was real blood. Since then, I've seen blood flow from the statue dozens of times.'

It is fashionable today to disbelieve in such things – or rather, to prefer to believe that such things do not happen. The closed or frightened mind characteristically takes refuge behind an exaggerated rationalism. To such entrenched sceptics, accounts of statues, paintings and other objects of religious worship seen weeping tears or issuing blood are evidence of the deplorable survival into this scientific age of primitive and superstitious beliefs. But there is evidence that proves such things do indeed happen at times, as the following stories show.

// IT BEGAN ON THE EVENING OF 16 MARCH 1960, WHEN A TINTED PORTRAIT OF THE BLESSED VIRGIN MARY BEGAN TO WEEP TEARS INSIDE ITS GLASS FRAME. THE TEARS DID NOT COLLECT BUT VANISHED. **//**

In the 1950s, an Italian physician, Dr Piero Casoli, made a prolonged study of weeping Madonnas. There was no shortage, for he concluded that they occurred on average about twice a year in Italy alone. And the records of the British *Fortean Times* show that such occurrences have been recorded throughout modern history, reports being received from all over the world. In 1527, for instance, a statue of Christ in Rome wept copiously and was taken as an omen of the fall of that city. In July 1966, a crucifix owned by Alfred Bolton of Walthamstow, London, shed tears on at least 30 occasions. In December 1960, a statue in a Greek

BLOOD AND TEARS

HOW CAN A PLASTER STATUE OF CHRIST SHED REAL BLOOD, OR A PAINTING OF THE VIRGIN CRY? THESE PHENOMENA HAVE BEEN RECORDED MANY TIMES, CONTINUING TO INSPIRE – AND ALSO PERPLEX – TODAY

One day in April 1975, just after Easter, Anne Poore of Boothwyn, Pennsylvania, USA, was praying for those who had turned away from the Church. She was kneeling in front of a 26-inch (66-centimetre) plaster statue of Jesus, given to her by a friend the year before. 'Suddenly I looked up at the statue,' she later told reporters, 'and my heart stopped beating. Two ruby-red drops of blood had appeared over the plaster wounds in its palms. I

The 300-year-old wooden crucifix, above, in the church at Porto das Caixas, Brazil, began to bleed in 1968. The carving then became the focus for many miraculous cures.

The crucifix, right, in the church of St Ignatius in Rome, was also seen to ooze drops of blood in 1959.

Orthodox church at Tarpon Springs, Florida, streamed 'little teardrops'. And in January 1981, a statue of the Virgin Mary at Caltanisetta, Sicily – said first to have wept in 1974 – began to bleed again from the right cheek.

Faced with such seemingly 'impossible' occurrences, we are prompted to ask the rational question: can these stories be dismissed as 'mass hallucinations'? There are certainly records of people gathered around a religious image said to bleed or weep, their anticipation fired by rumour, who have 'seen' the miracle, possibly when the most suggestible person present cried out: 'Look, the Madonna is weeping!' The American psychical researcher Raymond Bayless himself discovered just such a case.

It began on the evening of 16 March 1960, when a tinted portrait of the Blessed Virgin Mary began to weep tears inside its glass frame. It was owned by Pagora Catsounis of New York, who immediately called in her priest, Father George Papadeas, of St Paul's Greek Orthodox Church, Hempstead. He said:

'When I arrived, a tear was drying beneath the left eye. Then, just before our devotions ended, I saw another tear well in her left eye. It started as a small, round globule of moisture in the corner of the eye and slowly trickled down her face'.

At the bottom of the frame, the slow but steady trickle did not collect, as expected, but appeared to vanish before it had a chance to form a puddle.

WEEPING MADONNAS

In the first week, 4,000 people filed through Mrs Catsounis' apartment to stare and to pray, while tears flowed intermittently. The painting was subsequently transferred to St Paul's. Then, almost beyond belief, another weeping Madonna turned up in the family. It was owned by an aunt of Mrs Catsounis, Antonia Koulis. The circumstances seemed suspicious, but the phenomenon was vouched for by the Archbishop himself. The portrait was said to weep copiously; and when Father Papadeas let reporters handle it, the picture was still damp. Samples of the fluid were taken for analysis and found not to be human tears. This painting

The plaster statue, above, began to bleed from its hands in April 1975 in the home of Anne Poore of Boothwyn, Pennsylvania, USA. Thereafter the hands bled every Friday and the statue became the centre piece of a shrine.

Archbishop Takovos, of the Greek Orthodox Church of America, is seen below, inspecting an icon of the Virgin Mary, reported to have shed tears in the home of the Catsounis family in 1960.

Another weeping Madonna, below right, was discovered in the Catsounis' home within weeks of the first. This was found to shed an 'oily' substance.

was also enshrined in St Paul's. Mrs Koulis was given a replacement, and this too began to weep.

It was at this point that Raymond Bayless began his investigations, as reported in the magazine *Fate* in March 1966. Close examination of the surface of the painting revealed stains below the eyes that consisted of crystallised particles, something like those of a serum. The accumulations, being dried, had not moved downwards. When Bayless examined the image a second time, these raised 'tears' were still in the same place. He found no pinholes or other openings through which liquid could have been introduced into the central area of the painting, and stated:

'During our first visit . . . one woman, who was acting as interpreter, suddenly cried out that a new tear was descending from an eye. I looked immediately but in my opinion such was absolutely not the case. Some viewers and worshippers were convinced they saw tears appear and move on the surface of the icon while my friend and I were both present. On the other hand, we both were convinced, because of our careful examination, that . . . the tear was not liquid and did not flow or even descend a fraction of an inch'.

The case of Anne Poore's bleeding statue is quite different. When she recovered from her shock at its sudden bleeding, she made the statue the centre piece of a shrine on her front porch where a great many people saw it. On Fridays and holy days, the flow of blood was particularly strong, streaming downwards, in a cyclical recurrence that parallels the regular bleedings of some stigmatics. Eventually, the statue was moved to St Luke's Episcopalian Church at Eddystone, Pennsylvania, and installed on a platform 10 feet (3 metres) above the altar. Father Chester Olszewski, pastor of the church, said: 'It has bled as long as four hours. I know there can be no trickery. I have seen the palms dry, then, minutes later have observed droplets of blood welling out of the wounds.... Incredibly the blood seldom runs off the statue. Its robes are now encrusted with dried blood'. Another priest, Father Henry Lovett, said he came to see it as a sceptic and went away convinced it was a miracle. 'I've personally taken the hands off the statue – they are held in place by wooden dowels – and examined them. They're solid chalk. And the statue has bled profusely even as I watched.'

A

B

THE BLOOD OF CHRIST?

In this case, there is no doubt that a blood-like liquid flowed mysteriously from the sites of Christ's wounds on the statue. But was it actually blood? Dr Joseph Rovito, a respected Philadelphia physician, conducted his own investigation. X-rays revealed no trace of a reservoir or other trick mechanism concealed in the statue, but the result of the blood tests was not so straightforward. Although identified as human blood, the low red cell count was curious, and indicated great age. The fact that the

C

D

▮▮ I WAS ASTOUNDED. THE PHOTO OF BOB'S GRANDMOTHER WAS SOAKING WET, DRIPPING WITH A SMALL POOL OF WATER ... THE PHOTO DIDN'T DRY QUICKLY ... WHEN IT DID DRY, THE AREA ABOUT THE FACE REMAINED PUFFED, AS THOUGH THE WATER HAD ORIGINATED THERE AND RUN DOWNWARDS FROM THE EYES. ▮▮

In September 1911, a portrait of Christ in the church at Mirebeau-en-Poitou in France began to ooze blood (A). By Christmas of that year, blood was flowing from both palms, from the head and from the stylised heart (B). By March 1912, the blood was flowing copiously (C). The phenomenon seemed in some way connected with the parish priest, Abbé Vachère. Consecrated hosts bled as he blessed them and a nearby statue of the Virgin Mary wept. Much to his superiors' displeasure, he revelled in the attention of the pilgrims who flocked to witness the ever-increasing bleeding (D). Abbé Vachère was eventually excommunicated. Mysteriously, the portrait stopped bleeding at his death in 1915.

blood flowed quite a distance before coagulating indicated that it was fairly fresh, but fresh blood contains millions of red cells. Father Lovett, and other Catholics, jumped to the conclusion that this was actually the blood of Christ.

Such images are almost always objects of worship, and so the mysterious appearance of liquids on or near these images is bound to be interpreted in a religious context. But outside this context, there are almost identical accounts of a variety of related phenomena: bleeding tombstones, for instance; persistently wet or recurring bloodstains in a few haunted houses (evidence of a legendary murder, perhaps); or the constant distillation of substances such as clear oils or blood-like fluids that appear to come from the relics of some saints.

Once trickery and natural explanations, such as condensation, have been discounted, and the flow of blood has been established as not coming from inside the statue, then we have to accept that the liquid is appearing on the surface of the object, materialised there from an unknown source by the mysterious phenomenon of teleportation. The same probably applies to the appearance of tears on statues or icons. Yet appearances of these liquids are not random; in fact, they are remarkably consistent, for they restrict themselves to sites where either faith or legend leads us to expect miraculous happenings. Further consistency is observed in the association between bleeding and images of Christ, and weeping and images of the Virgin Mary. This regular association suggests either that the teleportative force is created by an unknown intelligence or that it acts automatically in response to especially powerful images in the human mind, on an instinctive or unconscious level.

American parapsychologist, D. Scott Rogo, told the story of the Reverend Robert Lewis who, on the day of his ordination, recalled how his grandmother – his first spiritual mentor – had wept with joy the day he said he wanted to join the ministry. However, she died before his ordination and he deeply regretted not being able to share the happiness of his success with her. He glanced at her photograph on his dresser, and suddenly accused his companion of playing a joke. The friend, the Reverend William Raucher, later wrote:

'I went over to see what was troubling him. I was astounded. The photo of Bob's grandmother was soaking wet, dripping with a small pool of water spreading on the dresser under it. Examining the picture we found that it was wet inside the glass.... The back of the picture, made of dyed imitation velvet, was so wet the velvet had streaked and faded. Removed from its frame, the photo didn't dry quickly. When it did dry, the area about the face remained puffed, as though the water had originated there and run downwards from the eyes'.

TEARS OF JOY

Rogo suggested that Lewis had unconsciously used a telekinetic ability to project a strong emotion into his immediate environment. 'Lewis underwent a mini-trauma when he passed his ordination exams,' wrote Rogo. 'His grandmother often wept with joy... He wanted to share his joy with [her]; he wanted to see her cry with happiness, so he used his psychic ability to stage the event.' Rogo made the further suggestion that this was not a freakish power of one individual, but that we all may possess this ability to cause dogmatic changes in our environment by projecting outside ourselves powerfully felt or suppressed emotions.

This type of paranormal projection, in which events are related to the spiritual or psychological tensions of those involved, takes two classic forms: overtly religious phenomena, and the disturbances known as poltergeist activity. In both cases, contemporary theorists relate the outburst of activity, or sudden manifestation of phenomena, to some inner crisis. Such a crisis may take many forms, such as the onset of puberty and its attendant physical and emotional complications, or the mounting pressures of illness, frustrations and inadequacies.

In May 1979, in New Mexico, for example, an ordinary plastic-coated, postcard-sized portrait of Jesus wept tears of seemingly genuine blood. The religious memento had been bought in 1972 by Kathy Malott for her grandmother, Willie Mae Seymore. On 25 May, Mrs Malott and her husband Zach were visiting Mrs Seymore when Mr Malott noticed a small dark drop forming on the picture, just under the right eye. It quickly turned into a steady stream, forming a puddle at the bottom, where it was tucked into the frame of a larger painting. 'The blood was running from the picture just as if I had cut my finger,' said Mrs Seymore. Mrs Malott went to wipe it off but, somewhat awed by the occurrence, other members of the family stopped her and decided to call a priest. One declined to come.

As the news spread, and reporters came to the house, many examined the postcard portrait and

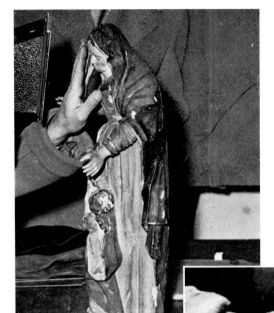

A finger of the statue of St Anne, left, belonging to Jean Salate, a hotel owner of Entrevaux in France, began to ooze blood, below, after Salate had broken it in a fit of anger in 1954. The finger bled 30 drops during the day and again the next morning. Crowds of the pious and the curious gathered to venerate the statue. Although chemical analysis proved that the blood was real, rumour soon spread that Salate had faked it.

The bronze statue of an aristocratic Japanese lady, below, owned by Allen Demetrius of Pittsburgh, USA, began to cry just 10 days before the nuclear accident at Three Mile Island, Pennsylvania in 1979. She had been known to weep only once before, on 6 August 1945, the night that an atomic bomb was dropped on Hiroshima. Demetrius said: 'It was like she was crying about the bombing'. Thousands of people travelled to witness the oxidised stains on the face of 'the weeping bronze of Hiroshima'.

could find no cut or hole through which a liquid could appear. The blood seemed to flow directly from the surface of the plastic. Later the substance was given a standard blood test – a 'hematest' – at the Eastern New Mexico Medical Center Hospital in Roswell. A spokesman said: 'Yes, it was honest-to-gosh bona fide blood'. An even more bizarre note was added when the blood was discovered still to be uncongealed after 24 hours.

Perhaps the most intriguing fact, however, was that the flow had only just begun when Zach Malott noticed it. It was almost as though the phenomenon was waiting for attention before it began in earnest.

SECOND COMING

There is an interesting sequel, too: four nights later, Zach Malott had a vivid dream in which Christ appeared and told him that the blood was a sign of his Second Coming. Prior to this, Malott had told reporters his family were 'not too religious'. Now, he said, his whole outlook had changed. 'I was sinner. Now I'm going to follow Jesus Christ.'

A more demonstrable case of bizarre cause and effect involves the celebrated weeping Madonna of Syracuse, Sicily. The statue was owned by Antonietta Janusso and was in fact a small plaster bust of the Virgin Mary in the style known as 'The Immaculate Heart of Mary' – a wedding gift, and a mass-produced ornament bought locally.

The couple were desperately poor and sharing accommodation in an extremely run-down quarter of the city. Suddenly, Mrs Janusso began to suffer mysterious illnesses. Some months into pregnancy, she experienced fits and convulsions, with alternating periods of blindness, deafness and dumbness. Doctors thought it was some kind of toxaemia but could find no cause. (However, similarity between her symptoms and those of clinical hysteria have been noted by some researchers.)

The bedridden girl, in a sorry state, looked up one day to the shelf above the bed where the statue rested, and saw it begin to cry. It continued to do so for many days and was seen by impeccable witnesses. But at the end of the first day, despite the excitement and strain of people crowding into the small room to see for themselves, Mrs Janusso felt considerably better, and by the time the statue had stopped crying, she had completely recovered.

▊▊ THE FLOW HAD ONLY JUST BEGUN WHEN ZACH MALOTT NOTICED IT. IT WAS ALMOST AS THOUGH THE PHENOMENON WAS WAITING FOR ATTENTION BEFORE IT BEGAN IN EARNEST... FOUR NIGHTS LATER, HE HAD A VIVID DREAM IN WHICH CHRIST APPEARED AND TOLD HIM THAT THE BLOOD WAS A SIGN OF HIS SECOND COMING. ▊▊

To the faithful, it was a miracle: to others, though, it seemed to be confirmation that her illnesses, genuinely debilitating though they were, had a hysterical origin. Indeed, perhaps the unconscious mind stages such apparently mystical or magical events in order to break a vicious circle of depression and self-pity. As has been said about the Catsounis case: 'The tears stopped when the reasons for self-pity were removed by blessing and return to health'.

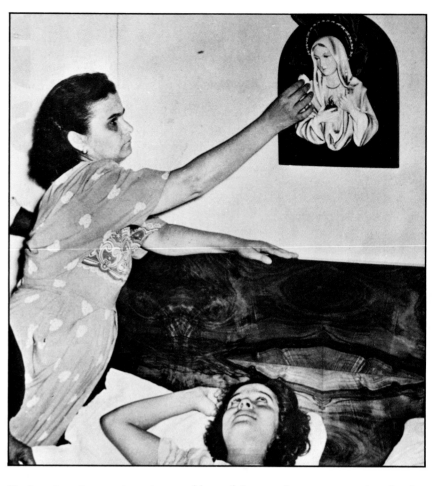

Mrs Antonietta Janusso, above, is seen lying on her sickbed in Syracuse, Sicily, in 1953 while her mother wipes away the tears shed by the plaster Madonna. She recovered completely after the statue stopped crying.

The Madonna of the Sicilian village of Caltanisetta, left, was seen to shed tears in 1974 and bled from a cheek in 1980. These 'flows' persisted under rigorous scrutiny.

Many of those unfortunate enough to be the focus of poltergeist phenomena also suffer from similar traumas, crises or changes. Mary Jobson, a 13-year-old poltergeist victim investigated in 1839 by Dr Reid Clanny, suffered patches of anaesthesia on her skin, as well as swellings, and convulsions, while her bedroom furniture moved, and while music and voices came from mid-air, and raps emanated from the walls. At times, quantities of water were also seen to fall, apparently from nowhere, on to the floor.

Many more cases could be cited, but one particularly worthy of mention seems to display overlapping characteristics of both the religious and the poltergeist type of projection. It centred on a devout 16-year-old Irish boy, James Walsh, of Templemore, Tipperary, in whose home all the holy pictures and statuary began to ooze blood. A hollow in the earthen floor of his room also kept filling with water, no matter how many times it was emptied. It was said that thousands of people took away containers of the water that was found there. The family was also tormented by mobile furniture and other forms of unexplained psychokinesis.

Such phenomena undoubtedly occur – but we can only guess at how or why. The facts are suggestive of a teleportation of liquids, but from where remains a mystery at present. Intriguing, too, is the difference between certain types of paranormal projection and the way in which they affect those who are troubled by them. As researcher Dr Nandor Fodor observed: 'Religious ecstasy of the weeping Madonna type restores, whereas the poltergeist senselessly frightens and destroys'.

DIVINING BY NUMBERS

USING NUMBERS IN ORDER TO DIVINE THE FUTURE OR INTERPRET CHARACTER OFTEN ANSWERS A DEEP-SEATED HUMAN NEED TO SEEK MEANING IN COMMONPLACE EVENTS. LEARN HOW TO CALCULATE YOUR OWN PERSONAL NUMBER, AS HIDDEN IN YOUR NAME, AND FIND OUT THE SECRETS THAT NUMEROLOGISTS BELIEVE IT HOLDS

Can the study of numbers reveal the future? Can they be used to reveal hidden aspects of a person's character? Practitioners of the ancient art of numerology believe they can.

Numerology is a method of making names, dates or events correspond to numbers – generally between one and nine, although sometimes 11 and 22 are included in the system. Each number has a certain significance: William Shakespeare, for instance, corresponds to five, the number of versatility and resourcefulness.

The correspondence is established by a very simple identification of the letters of the alphabet with numbers according to the 'Hebrew system', as numerologists call it, and as illustrated in the table below..

To find your number, simply write down the number corresponding to each letter of your name, and add them together. If the resulting number is over nine, add up its digits and keep doing this until the result is less than 10. For instance, the letters of the name Charlotte Brontë add to five. (Charlotte = 3 + 5 + 1 + 2 + 3 + 7 + 4 + 4 + 5 = 34; Brontë = 2 + 2 + 7 + 5 + 4 + 5 = 25; 34 + 25 = 59; 5 + 9 = 14; 1 + 4 = 5.)

If the digits corresponding to your name add up to one, you are probably a dominant kind of person, a leader. 'Ones' are pioneers, inventors, designers – but they often put their plans into practice with little regard for the way they will affect those most directly involved. They tend to dominate everyone they meet, rarely have close friends and are sometimes, despite their confident appearance, very lonely people.

Two is interpreted by modern numerologists as the number of passive, receptive people. 'Twos' are quiet, unambitious, gentle, kind, tidy and conscientious. They often get their own way, however, by gentle persuasion rather than force. They are inclined to be hesitant, and to make problems for themselves by putting off decisions for no good reason. This quality can sometimes lead them into difficult situations.

In Albrecht Dürer's engraving Melencolia I (1514), below, the artist has included a magic square in the upper right-hand corner, its rows, columns and diagonals of numbers all adding up to the same total. Such squares, epitomising the mystical properties of numbers, have often been used as talismans.

The table, below left, is that most generally used by numerologists to calculate the number corresponding to a particular name or word.

THE 'HEBREW' NUMEROLOGICAL SYSTEM

1	2	3	4	5	6	7	8
A	B	C	D	E	U	O	F
I	K	G	M	H	V	Z	P
Q	R	L	T	N	W		
J		S			X		
Y							

Traditionally, three is one of the most extrovert numbers, belonging to intelligent, creative and witty people, who generally make friends easily and seem to succeed at anything to which they turn their hands. They are proud, ambitious and pleasure-loving, but their great weakness lies in an inability to take anything – ideas or people – seriously for very long.

Four, like two, is a number corresponding to dependable, down-to-earth people. They are born organisers. They lack the volatility of 'ones' and 'threes', but they make up for this by fairness and meticulous attention to detail. They may be subject to sudden irrational rages or depressions that seem extraordinary in people who are usually models of calmness. Four has also long been regarded by numerologists as the number of ill-luck; indeed, those whose number is four often seem to pay dearly for any success they achieve in life.

Five is the number of bright, fast-moving, clever, impatient people. They live on their nerves, and love meeting people and seeking out new experiences. They are often physically attractive but rather feckless, hating to be tied down. Five is the number that represents sex (the digits of which also add up to five), and people whose number is five often have varied and exciting love-lives that can be problematic. Sometimes the sexual side of their nature may even show itself in excesses or perversions.

People whose number is six are among the happiest of the whole numerological system. They are happy, tranquil, well-balanced and home-loving. They are affectionate, loyal, sincere and conscientious. They are often creative, and many of them are successful in the performing arts. The negative aspect of their character is a tendency to be rather fussy, conceited and self-satisfied.

Seven is the number of the loner, the introspective scholar, philosopher, mystic or occultist. These people tend to stand aside from the mainstream of life, content to observe it. They are dignified, self-controlled and reserved. They tend to be indifferent to worldly wealth but, while they may seem aloof and stand-offish, make loyal friends. Despite their powerful intellects, they are often surprisingly bad at putting their thoughts into words, and may even dislike discussing them if they feel their own ideas are being challenged.

Eight represents worldly success, people who have this number often making successful businessmen, politicians or lawyers. Their success is, however, often built on a great deal of hard work, likely to be done at considerable expense to their warmer, more human qualities. They often seem to be hard, egocentric and grasping; but behind the unsympathetic exterior, there can be a whimsical streak that endears them to other people.

Nine stands for the height of intellectual and spiritual achievement. People whose number is nine are the idealists, the romantics, the visionaries – poets, missionaries, doctors, religious teachers, brilliant scientists. Their great qualities are unselfishness, self-discipline and determination and their idealism is concerned with mankind as a whole. In their everyday lives, they may be inclined to seek the limelight, and to be fickle friends or lovers, however.

Some numerologists also employ the numbers 11 and 22. They believe that these represent a higher plane of experience than the numbers one to nine. Eleven is the number of those who experience revelations and suffer martyrdom; those with names that add up to this number are often people with a strong vocation for their work – preachers, doctors, nurses or teachers. They tend to be idealists in many respects.

Twenty-two, meanwhile, is the 'master' number; and people whose names add to 22 combine the best qualities of all the other numbers.

The number of New York, seen below, is three – representing pride, ambition and love of pleasure, but an inability to take ideas and people seriously for long. Some would find this an apt description of the USA's glittering capital of finance and fashion.

PERSPECTIVES

MYSTICAL NUMBERS

In the 16th century, the Western esoteric tradition – witchcraft, alchemy and astrology, for example – began to be influenced by a complex Jewish mystical system known as the *Kabbala* (Hebrew for 'tradition'), much of it concerned with the power and meaning of numbers in the Hebrew scriptures.

Since, in Hebrew, each letter also represents a number, Kabbalists would, for example, take a Hebrew word from the Bible, translate each letter into a number, add them up and then find another word with letters adding up to the same total. These words, they claimed, had a mystical connection with each other.

Kabbalists also enjoyed speculating on biblical passages containing actual numbers. The measurements of Noah's Ark, for instance, was thought to be imbued with meaning as to God's nature, even reflecting the anatomy of Adam Kadmon, the archetypal human in whose image mankind was supposedly created.

The ground-plan at the heart of the Kabbalistic system is the Tree of Life – a geometrical arrangement of ten spheres, the so-called *sefirot,* each of which is associated with a divine attribute (such as Wisdom and Mercy), and 22 paths connecting the spheres.

The study of the Hebrew letters, with their corresponding numbers, their inner meaning and position on the 22 paths of the Tree of Life, is said to give Kabbalists a key to understanding how the creation originally came about.

Eleven is the number of those with a strong sense of vocation – such as Churchill, left, and Florence Nightingale, far left. Albert Einstein, below left, even called himself a 'lone traveller'. What Pablo Picasso, below, was told by his mother could be said of any of them: 'If you become a soldier, you'll be a general. If you become a monk, you'll end up as the Pope'.

Apply this procedure to the name you were given at birth and you find, numerologists claim, the characteristics you were born with and that will underlie your personality throughout your life; apply it to the name you give yourself, or would like to have, and you will discover how your experiences in the world have moulded your personality. Using a nickname, you will be able to ascertain what your friends think of you. Comparing her maiden and married names, a married woman can find out how married life is likely to have changed her.

HIDDEN NUMBERS

The total of vowel numbers in your name is your heart number, which shows your inner character. The total of consonants is your personality number, which indicates your outward personality, or the impression you make on the people around you. (This distinction is derived from Hebrew, in which only the consonants of any word are actually written down; the vowels are therefore 'hidden', and represent the aspects of the personality that are not outwardly apparent.)

Numerologists believe that numbers can also be used to suggest beneficial courses of action. If your number is seven, for example, you should be sure to make difficult decisions or perform important tasks on days of the month that add up to seven: that is, the seventh, the 16th and the 25th. Certain years, too, can be good or bad for an individual. To find your year-number, add your month and date of birth to the current year: 1992, for instance, is a 2-year for someone born on 24 February (24 + 2 + 1992 = 2018; 2 + 0 + 1 + 8 = 11; 1 + 1 = 2), indicating it is a year for quiet reflection and gentle action, rather then forcefulness.

Why, though, should the system work? Numerologists are quick to point out instances that seem to show the importance of number, such as in the career of Louis XIV of France. He came to the

throne in 1643, which adds up to 14; he died in 1715, which adds up to 14, at the age of 77 – which adds up to 14. But is it just coincidence?

Numerologists counter this question by claiming that there is no such thing as coincidence. They believe the Universe is like a vast harp with countless strings, each vibrating at a certain rate, characterised by a number. Number, they believe, is at the root of all things. They point out, too, that science has found that light, sound, atomic structure and many other things are dependent on frequency, or number. But what of the objection that, even if this view of the Universe is correct, basing the system on a person's name must be wrong, since the naming of a child is largely a matter of the personal tastes and whims of the parents? The numerologists have their answers ready, as Florence Campbell, an American, explains:

'The Soul has taken many journeys in the past and knows its present needs. The Soul wants progress upwards on the Great Spiral and chooses for the incarnating ego the vowels whose total shall accomplish this purpose... There is a long "Dark Cycle" before the child is born, and during this Dark Cycle the vibrations that are to label the new life are so impressed upon the subconscious minds of the parents that they are compelled to carry out the plan.'

In other words, the numerologist believes that the name each person carries is no accident, and that it tells something significant about its bearer, in a code to which the numerologist has the key.

Like the character types suggested by the sign of the zodiac under which you were born, the traits indicated by these numbers are to be regarded as indicating a general type, not a detailed description. But that people whose names add to the same number share certain personality traits can be supported with numerous examples. The letters of the names Winston S. Churchill, Einstein, Pablo Picasso and Florence Nightingale, for instance, all add up to 11 – the number belonging to those with strong vocations in life.

The same technique can be applied to the names of cities, and many of the results seem to confirm the beliefs of numerologists. London adds up to five, indicating many-sidedness and resilience; New York to three, indicating brilliance and glitter. The ancient cities of Oxford and Cambridge both have the number seven – the number of the aloof, inwardly-turned scholar.

Numerology can also be used to assess the characteristic of a year, decade or century. The 1920s, depicted top, the third decade of the century, had the number three – the number of the pleasure-loving and fickle; but the 1930s, centre, corresponded to four, representing unstable moods and ill-luck. (The decade began with the Depression – a Christmas Day dole queue is shown here – and ended with the Second World War.) After VE Day, above, the 1940s saw the return of prosperity and renewed experiment in fashions and life-styles – in character with the decade's number five ('bright, clever, impatient').

ALTHOUGH ROMAN CATHOLICISM IS NOMINALLY THE PREVAILING RELIGION OF BRAZIL, LIFE THERE EVEN TODAY IS INTERWOVEN WITH THE PAGAN AND MAGICAL ELEMENTS OF ANCIENT SPIRIT CULTS THAT ARE AFRICAN IN ORIGIN

A massive statue of Christ, left, towers over Rio de Janeiro. Although Brazil's official religion is Roman Catholicism, many of the country's inhabitants also adhere to the beliefs of Macumba, the Brazilian form of voodoo. Rio's Copacabana beach, below, is both a pleasure resort and the scene of many Macumba rites, such as the one shown here in honour of the African sea goddess Yemanja.

Brazil has a population of around 145 million and is often described as the world's largest Catholic country. Nominally this is true: almost every child born in the country is baptised, and most Brazilians receive the last rites of the Church when they are mortally ill and, after death, a Catholic funeral. But while the Catholic churches are often crowded, the voodoo temples of *Candomblé*, *Umbanda* and other Afro-American spirit religions (in Brazil, collectively referred to as *Macumba*) are more crowded still.

The practice of *Macumba* rituals is widespread throughout the country and does not take place only inside temples. *Macumba* ceremonies are performed in isolated clearings in the the Amazonian jungle, at crossroads (traditionally, as in Europe, popular places for magic rites), and even on Rio de Janeiro's famous Copacabana beach, which is one of the world's most popular pleasure spots.

This dual role of Copacabana beach aptly illustrates the powerful hold that Afro-American religion and magic have on Brazilian life. By day, the beach is packed with sunbathing tourists; by night, it is thronged with *Macumbistas* worshipping a host of exotic gods and demons, and casting spells designed to obtain love, money or power, or even the death of an enemy.

On New Year's Eve, Copacabana is the site of a major *Macumba* festival combining secular, religious and magical elements, at which the gods of pagan Africa are worshipped, together with the Catholic saints with whom they are identified. The principal object of adoration, however, is the African sea goddess Yemanja, who is often identified with the Virgin Mary.

DRUMMING UP THE SPIRITS

Yemanja was brought to Brazil by Yoruba slaves from the area of Africa that is now Nigeria. In Yoruba mythology, Yemanja was the daughter of heaven and earth. She married her brother, and then coupled with her son, who fathered on her a whole tribe of gods and goddesses, among them Shango, the god of storm and thunder (identified by *Macumbistas* with St John the Baptist); Ogun, the god of war and iron-working; and Orishako, a peasant god who rules over agriculture and female fertility. The name Yemanja is derived from the Yoruba words for 'mother' and 'fish': she is the 'mother of all fish' and therefore queen of the ocean and everything under and upon it. For this reason, her chief festival is held on the seashore, and the offerings dedicated to her are given to the sea.

As sunset approaches on 31 December, *Macumbistas* make their way individually or in small groups to Copacabana beach. Some come on foot, some in cars (many of *Macumba*'s devotees belong to the prosperous middle classes). And since the New Year's Eve festival is of national significance, many more come in motor coaches from temples hundreds of miles away.

The worshippers are mostly dressed in white – Yemanja's favourite colour – and they carry candles and gifts to be offered to the goddess. Each devotee places lighted candles in a previously dug hole that is carefully walled with sand as a protection against the wind. The offerings – which can take many forms, including mirrors, bottles of scent, hair ribbons or, in the case of prosperous businessmen, expensive bottles of imported Bourbon – are placed nearby.

Each devotee then looks fixedly into the flames of the flickering candles and asks Yemanja for some favour. The more candles there are, the better: it seems that either Yemanja likes the smell of burning wax, or she wants her worshippers to spend as much money as possible to show their devotion.

On Copacabana beach at night, top, a priestess dedicates flowers, clothing and other items to Yemanja before consigning them to the waves.

David St Clair, above, was the victim of 'closing the paths', a particular technique of Quimbanda black magic.

At the Saída dos Santos ceremony, which celebrates the 'leaving of the saints', left, a dancer dressed in rich ceremonial robes represents the voodoo deity Oxum.

Whether the number of candles offered is odd or even is also important. If the devotee wants some material benefit, such as a wage increase or a new car, he must burn an even number of candles: for something to do with the emotions, such as a love affair or a better relationship with one's neighbours, the number must be odd. If the candles burn to extinction or are swept out to sea by the incoming tide, it is a sign the wish will be granted. If, however, they are blown out by the wind, the omen is unfavourable.

ORGIASTIC DANCE

As the myriads of candles are lit, the *Macumba* drums start to sound, and the dancing begins. At first, only a few people dance, rather mechanically, as if performing a necessary but boring duty. But as the evening wears on, the numbers increase, and a frenzied, almost orgiastic, quality becomes apparent. Eventually, as in the voodoo celebrations of Haiti, some of the dancers enter a trance state and become possessed: the gods descend and 'mount their horses'.

As in Haiti, those who are possessed seem to lose all consciousness of their own identity. When they return to normal consciousness, they cannot remember what happened during trance. Out of the great number of dancers on the beach, only a few will achieve this state: nevertheless, it is possible for the interested onlooker to move through the crowds and meet many members of the *Macumba* pantheon, such as the god of war, the god of thunder, 'the Old Black Slave' (a supernatural being, renowned for his powers of healing), or Exu, a sinister entity who is the nearest *Macumba* equivalent to Satan.

In due time, the tide sweeps away Yemanja's gifts, the entranced dancers return to normal consciousness, the worshippers make their way homewards, and the festival is over for another year.

But the New Year's Eve festival at Copacabana is no mere anachronistic survival from a past age of slavery and superstition. Belief in the existence of the spirit world is alive and well at every level of

Brazilian society. Peasants, factory hands, bankers and politicians – almost all believe in gods, demons and supernatural powers, even if they are not prepared to admit it to sceptical foreigners. This widespread acceptance of the supernatural would seem to extend even to such a prosaic institution as the Brazilian Post Office. In 1957 and 1964, it issued pictorial stamps in honour of *The Spirits' Book* and *The Gospel According to Spiritism*, both works by Allan Kardec, the founding father and first theoretician of Spiritism.

Kardec's Spiritism incorporates a belief in reincarnation, and its influence on *Macumba* varies from group to group. Some temples conduct ceremonies that are almost completely 'Kardecised'. When the devotees are in a state of trance, they follow a Europeanised pattern of behaviour and their actions are quite as restrained and unalarming as those of any French or English Spiritualist medium. In other temples that are less influenced by Kardec, however, those possessed by the gods will engage in remarkable and spectacular activities that are seen by the onlookers as evidence of genuine control by otherworldly beings. Such activities have been seen to include walking on broken bottles, inserting large needles into the cheeks, fire-eating, and drinking whole bottles of raw cane spirit within the space of a few minutes, all apparently without any untoward effect.

Yet manifestations of this kind are not as uncontrolled as they may appear. *Macumba* ceremonies follow a pattern that is quite as predictable, in terms of its own conventions, as any Christian service.

Brazilian **Macumba** *ceremonies are folk rituals in which all present participate to some degree. At the climax of a festival,* **above,** *dancers are seen prostrating themselves.*

The young girl, **below,** *dances vigorously in a trance to rhythmic hand-clapping and music played on simple instruments.*

Stylised drum rhythms, dancing, a charged atmosphere of religious expectation, and the practice of deliberate over-breathing (which produces changes in brain chemistry) induce a near-hypnotic state in all the participants. Finally, when the high priestess calls down the gods, the dancers stop moving one by one. Some of them bend down, and then straighten up, often with a scream, in a trance, supposedly possessed by a divinity.

CLOSING THE PATHS

But as in Haiti, so in Brazil there is a darker side to spirit religion. This is *Quimbanda*, an evil voodoo in which practitioners work black magic against their own and, for a fee, their clients' enemies. A favourite technique of *Quimbanda* is 'closing the paths'. This involves casting a spell that blocks the victim's progress to personal happiness. The person who has been subjected to this finds that love and financial matters cause nothing but trouble, that his physical and mental health deteriorate, and that problems arise for him in even the most ordinary everyday affairs.

The American writer David St Clair seems to have been the victim of just such a psychic attack during the time he lived in Brazil. First, his girlfriend left him, and money he was expecting did not arrive. Then, legal difficulties arose over an inheritance, and he contracted malaria. He attributed all this misfortune to nothing more sinister than bad luck – until, that is, a Brazilian friend, a *Macumbista* who claimed to have psychic powers, told him that 'his paths had been closed' by *Quimbanda*.

At first, St Clair thought this was superstitious nonsense. Soon afterwards, however, he received a message from a Spiritualist source: his maid, Edna, had employed black magic against him. Each week, it was alleged, she took an item of his clothing to a *Quimbanda* ceremony. There, it was buried while 'crossing spells' were chanted and ceremonial candles burned around it. In addition, said the Spiritualist, Edna was adding a magical 'closing powder' to his food. St Clair was still sceptical, but he had seen too many strange things in Brazil to discount completely the idea that black magic was being used against him. He decided to fight fire with fire, and to attend a *Macumba* ceremony himself, so that he could consult one of the possessed.

The votive offerings, right, have been dedicated to a deity to effect a cure. The images themselves (such as the feet and breast in the foreground), or a mark on an image, indicate the parts of the body that need to be healed.

The first part of the ceremony he attended followed the conventional pattern of drumming, dancing and possession. But then something extraordinary happened. The priestess, who was wearing the customary *Macumba* vestments and regalia – a spotlessly white blouse and skirt with a gold cross at her breast – suddenly left the temple. When she returned a few minutes later, her appearance was completely different. She was clad in filthy red satin tatters; and in place of the golden cross was the skull of a human infant, its jaws tied together with black tape, a dead snake wreathed between the staring eye sockets.

Rituals and dances often take place at night and can last for hours. Fatigue is evident on the faces of the followers, below, who urge on dancers with their rhythmic clapping.

Laughing insanely, the priestess seized a bottle of rum, gulped half of it down, and announced that she was Exu, the *Macumba* equivalent of Satan.

A long conversation ensued between St Clair, 'Exu' and two mediums, one of whom was possessed by 'Satan's dog'. Eventually 'Exu', who claimed he sometimes did good as well as evil, told St Clair: 'The curse has been lifted, and will come down doubly on the person who placed it on you.'

Within a few days 'the paths opened' for St Clair. His psychological attitude changed for the better and, perhaps because he no longer expected the worst, his health, finances and love-life all improved. Possession of a priestess by a voodoo deity had transformed his outlook on life.

This, perhaps, is the real power of voodoo, *Macumba* and other Afro-American spirit religions. Indeed, it is possible that possession by the gods offers the devotee something of greater therapeutic value to a diseased psyche than do orthodox Western remedies.

" BRAZIL HAS MADE A NAME FOR ITSELF IN RECENT YEARS AS A LAND OF PARANORMAL PHENOMENA... IT MIGHT BE HELPFUL FOR VISITORS TO HAVE SIGNS PUT UP OUTSIDE SÃO PAULO'S CONGONHAS AIRPORT SUCH AS: WARNING! YOU ARE ENTERING A POLTERGEIST ZONE, MATERIALISATIONS TWICE NIGHTLY, OR SIMPLY WELCOME TO THE CAPITAL OF ESP. *"*

GUY PLAYFAIR, THE FLYING COW

The French occultist Alphonse-Louis Constant, better known as the magical writer Eliphas Lévi, is seen right, as a young man. Constantly searching for a cause, Lévi had devoted himself to the Church, and then to revolutionary politics; but it was only when he met the exiled Polish mystic J. M. Hoene-Wronski, below right, that he found his life's work, and eventually became the world's foremost ritual magician.

ELIPHAS LEVI - RITUAL MAGICIAN

MODERN STUDENTS OF THE OCCULT OFTEN CITE THE 19TH-CENTURY FRENCH WRITER ELIPHAS LÉVI AS AN AUTHORITY ON MAGIC. BUT THERE IS EVIDENCE TO SHOW THAT HE FREQUENTLY EXAGGERATED MANY OF HIS MORE NOTABLE 'ACHIEVEMENTS'

At the present day, almost every great city of the Western world has a Polish community, comprising men and women exiled from their homeland because of opposition to a former Polish government and its one-time Russian masters. The situation was similar throughout much of the 19th century. Numbers of these exiles lived in Paris: some took refuge in political plotting, others in mystical dreams, seeing Poland as the 'Messiah nation', a sacrificial victim whose sufferings would redeem the rest of Europe.

Among the latter was J.M. Hoene-Wronski (1776-1853), perhaps the oddest dreamer of them all, and the first occult teacher to inspire the French writer who called himself Eliphas Lévi. Wronski was originally a soldier by profession, but abandoned the military life for philosophy and science, and made his way to France, where he supported himself by teaching mathematics. By 1810, he had come to believe that he had 'discovered the Absolute' – in other words, that he had reached, through reason, a perfect understanding of the nature of ultimate reality and truth. He expressed this supposed 'understanding' in mathematical formulae that proved incomprehensible not only to laymen but to other mathematicians. Nevertheless, so convinced was he of his own genius that he visited London in order to petition Parliament for grants and subsidies. Here, he made such a nuisance of himself that one distinguished mathematician, a member of the scientific committee known as the Board of Longitude, stated that: 'in the interests of social order, one must hope that Wronski will one night go to bed and not wake up again the next day.' This gentleman's distaste for Wronski would probably have been even stronger if he had realised that the Polish savant was also an occultist and mystic, a student of such strange subjects as Gnosticism and the Kabbalah, who believed that, by means of mystical processes, ordinary human beings could attain God-like powers.

In 1850, Wronski met Alphonse-Louis Constant (1810-1875), better known as Eliphas Lévi, a hack journalist who had once trained for the priesthood but had lost his faith, who had dabbled in revolutionary politics and become disillusioned, and who was looking for a new set of beliefs that would give meaning to a purposeless existence. To Lévi – to use the name he adopted – Wronski expounded his doctrine of the Absolute, his belief that Poland was 'the Christ of Europe', his interpretations of the

In the depiction below, Lévi undertakes the supreme magical rite – the evocation to visible appearance of the 1st-century sage, Apollonius of Tyana. After lengthy and peculiar preparations, Lévi evoked Apollonius three times on consecutive days in order to ask the spirit profound questions on the nature of the Universe. The apparition is said to have complied; but unfortunately Lévi did not record the conversations.

Kabbalah and other mystical systems, and his belief that, through the practice of ritual magic, men could attain semi-divinity.

Lévi was captivated. He threw himself into the study of all the 'occult sciences', from alchemy to cartomancy (telling fortunes with playing cards), and from magic to astrology. He rifled the libraries of Paris for esoteric books and manuscripts, reading them voraciously, and spent many hours with obscure soothsayers, diviners, magicians and self-appointed prophets, hoping to extract wisdom from his long and often pointless conversations with them. He also came to believe that the ancient texts of alchemy and magic were written in a symbolic code; and that if he could only break this code, he would learn the ultimate secrets of the Universe and become the custodian of certain spiritual truths, beside which the discoveries and interpretations of Wronski would pale into insignificance.

In 1853, Wronski died, ostensibly mourned – but not, in truth, deeply regretted – by Lévi who, by this time, believed that he had already surpassed the skills of his former master and was well on the way to receiving some great spiritual revelation.

A year later, in 1854, he decided that his researches were sufficiently advanced for him to carry out an important occult experiment – the evocation to visible appearance of the spirit of Apollonius of Tyana, a philosopher and wonder-worker of the first century.

Lévi recorded that he prefaced this rite by three weeks of preparation and purification. During

*In*Focus

INFERNAL EVOCATIONS

Eliphas Lévi, who was born in 1810, grew up and spent his adult life in a period characterized by an all-pervading romanticism – which often degenerated into a frantic search for the merely picturesque or, by contrast, the abnormal.

By the time Lévi had reached the age of 30, the Romantic movement dominated the cultural life of France – and Lévi, too, was ensnared by it, being a man with a desperate need to believe. Indeed, he could not face the world without holding up some ideological banner, inscribed with 'the truth'.

The nature of this 'truth' changed as Lévi grew older. As an adolescent, he had found it in romanticized Catholicism, and as a young man in an equally romanticized revolutionary Socialism; and for his last 20 years or so, in a grossly distorted, 'picturesque' interpretation of the bizarre practices of the occult tradition of the Western world.

This was shaped by Lévi's wide reading, uncritical acceptance of the assertions of a number of unscholarly historians, and his remarkable capacity for self-deception (shared by the occultist Aleister Crowley, this time, he restricted his activities to eating nothing but vegetables, avoiding other people, and carrying on long, imaginary conversations with the long dead sage.

The preparations over, Lévi – clad in white vestments and wearing on his head a wreath of vervain entwined with a golden chain – began the ceremony by lighting charcoal fires in two copper chafing dishes. On these, he burned various types of incense, their heavy smoke designed to provide the material from which the spirit of the philosopher could build himself a 'body'. Lévi began to read the words of the ritual he was employing. Then, as he stated:

'The smoke spread... floating above the altar... I heaped more fuel and perfume upon the chafing dishes... I beheld distinctly before the altar, the figure of a man of more than normal size... Three times, with closed eyes, I invoked Apollonius. When I again looked, there was a man in front of me, wrapped from head to foot in a shroud... I experienced an abnormally cold sensation, and when I endeavoured to question the phantom, I could not utter a syllable. I... pointed my magic sword at the figure, mentally commanding it to obey me... The form became vague and suddenly vanished. I ordered it to return and presently felt, as it were, a breath close by me; something touched the hand with which I was holding the sword, and immediately my forearm became numb. I guessed that the sword displeased the spirit, and I placed its point downward, close by me, within the circle... I experienced such a weakness in all my limbs, and a fainting sensation came so quickly over me, that I sat down, whereupon I fell into a profound lethargy accompanied by dreams of which I had only a confused recollection when I recovered... '

The spirit of Apollonius did not speak to Lévi, but the answers to the two questions he had intended to ask it – one on behalf of a friend, one on his own account – came into his mind. The reply to the friend, who had asked about someone's health, was 'Death'; the answer to his own (unrecorded) question was similarly gloomy.

VERY SECRET SECRETS

Over the next few days, Lévi twice more evoked Apollonius. Each time, claimed Lévi, the sage appeared and gave profound philosophical answers to Lévi's equally profound questions. Unfortunately, the exact wording, of neither the questions propounded nor the answers received, was recorded, so it is impossible to estimate the truth of Lévi's claim that Apollonius revealed secrets 'which might change, in a short time, the foundations and laws of society at large, if they became generally known'.

If the secrets were, indeed, as astonishing as Lévi claimed, it is rather remarkable that he proceeded to warn others against carrying out similar occult experiments. He wrote:

'... I regard the practice as destructive and dangerous... I commend the greatest caution to those who propose devoting themselves to similar experiences; their result is intense exhaustion, and frequently a shock sufficient to occasion illness.'

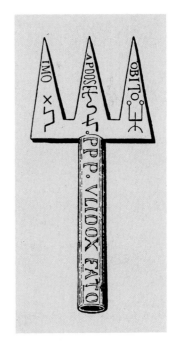

Lévi's version of the 'trident of Paracelsus' to which he attributed extraordinary Kabbalistic significance, is shown above. However, his misreading of the ancient texts had led him astray; Paracelsus merely regarded the trident as a device for curing sexual impotence that had been brought about by witchcraft.

who actually believed he was the reincarnation of Lévi, whom he eclipsed in learning).

Lévi's written statements regarding the many surviving printed and manuscript grimoires – medieval and Renaissance textbooks of ritual magic – typified his whole attitude. When he quoted from these works, he did so selectively and inaccurately, picking out (and heavily amending) passages that were sufficiently romantic to read as though extracted from a particularly lurid Gothic novel. If no passages in any extant grimoire were sufficiently dramatic to suit his purposes, he would resort to invention.

Take, for example, Lévi's description of the processes involved in 'infernal evocations' – the raising of the denizens of hell to visible appearance. The sorcerer begins, said Lévi, with 15 days of a curious dietary observance – getting totally drunk every five days on wine in which hemp and poppy have been infused and which has been strained through a cloth woven by a prostitute. The actual evocation should be carried out in a haunted graveyard or 'the vaults of an abandoned convent' – both, significantly enough, popular settings for Gothic novels.

Among other essential requirements for the ceremony were, claimed Lévi, such bizarre items as 'the head of a black cat which had fed on human flesh for five days, four nails from the coffin of an executed criminal, and the horns of a goat that had experienced sexual intercourse with a young girl' (shown in a magical design, the symbolic circle, reproduced *left*). All this is very melodramatic, but almost none of it was actually derived from the grimoires that were, according to Lévi, its supposed sources.

Lévi's imagination made his books very readable – but valueless, it turns out, as serious studies of the occult tradition.

Lévi's design for the Great Seal of Solomon, sometimes known as the Double Triangle of Solomon, *left*, *shows the magician's acknowledgement of the duality of all things – with the good shown above and the evil below.*

Not many months after his raising of the ghost of Apollonius to visible appearance, Lévi published a book entitled *The Dogma of High Magic.* In this and its sequel, *The Ritual of High Magic,* published two years later, Lévi presented what he claimed to be an accurate account of the theory and practice of alchemy, ceremonial magic, divination and the other 'occult sciences'. In reality, these treatises are often grossly inaccurate where matters of fact are concerned. Many of his definitive statements are, quite simply, erroneous. Some of these errors were probably the result of carelessness in the use of manuscripts and other primary sources – Lévi was a widely, but not deeply, read man; and others can be attributed to deliberate distortion for no other purpose than the production of exciting reading. A particularly gross example is provided by Lévi's account of 'the Trident of Paracelsus', a three-pronged fork inscribed with various mystic symbols. Lévi asserted that the three prongs represented both the Christian Trinity of Father, Son and Holy Ghost and the alchemical elements (principles) of salt, sulphur and mercury.

The trident expressed, Lévi added:

'... the synthesis of the Trinity in Unity... Paracelsus ascribed to it all the virtues which Kabbalistic Hebrews attribute to the Name of Jehovah and the thaumaturgic [magical] properties of ABRACADABRA, used by the hierophants of Alexandria.'

All this is unmitigated rubbish. Paracelsus certainly wrote of this trident; but equally certainly, he did not attribute to it all the virtues of 'the Name of Jehovah' – rather, he regarded it as a device to be used for the cure of sexual impotence brought about by witchcraft. According to Paracelsus, those inflicted in this way should make a trident from an old horseshoe 'on the Day of Venus and in the Hour of Saturn', inscribe it with various occult symbols, and conceal it in the bed of a running stream. 'By this means,' wrote Paracelsus, 'thou shalt be delivered in nine days and the person that has brought this mischief upon thee shall get something himself in that place [the genitals].' All this is very interesting, no doubt, but it is a long way from Levi's 'synthesis of the 'Trinity in Unity' and 'the thaumaturgic properties of Abracadabra'.

DESIGNS UPON THE TAROT

At times, Lévi did more than distort the facts – he invented them to suit his purpose. He wanted, for example, to prove that the Tarot cards were known to, and employed by, occultists of the 16th and 17th centuries. He therefore specifically stated that there were references to the Tarot in the writings of such men as Abbot Trithemius, the 16th-century scholar, and Knorr von Rosenroth, the 17th-century Kabbalist. In truth, there are no such references.

Inaccuracies of this sort flawed all the literary work of Lévi. Anyone who looks for reliable accounts of the history of Western occultism and the techniques employed by its devotees must seek elsewhere than in the writings of the French magician.

Nevertheless, Lévi's theories as to how magic supposedly works cannot be neglected. For not only are they interesting in their own right, they have inspired whole generations of occultists, including Madame H.P. Blavatsky and the renowned magician Aleister Crowley.

As far as Lévi was concerned, three fundamental theories – which he called 'dogmas' – explain all allegedly supernatural phenomena, from miraculous healings, apparently induced by holy relics, to the table-turning of Spiritualist mediums.

The first of these theories is the 'dogma of correspondence', an idea of great antiquity. According to this, the soul of a human being is a microcosm, a little Universe that properly reflects in miniature the

nature of the macrocosm, the great Universe in which we live. Every factor in the Universe has its counterpart in the soul and, by means of traditional occult practices, according to this dogma, the magician can change the world outside himself by changing the little world inside.

THE ASTRAL LINK

The link between the inner and outer worlds is the 'astral light', an invisible but all pervading substance whose existence forms the basis of the second of Levi's dogmas. According to Lévi, this astral (literally 'starry') light has a close relationship to matter, each physical object having an astral twin. By manipulating the astral light, it is possible, said Lévi, for the occultist to influence both physical phenomena (to tip tables or heal the sick, for example) and the feelings and modes of consciousness of other living beings.

This manipulation can be achieved by the trained human imagination and will. Indeed, Lévi's third fundamental theory is that will and imagination are real, natural forces, capable – when properly harnessed – of producing even more spectacular effects than those produced by, say, electricity.

During his lifetime, Lévi's theories attracted little attention. His books sold only moderately, and he eked out a scanty living by taking 'occult pupils'. Many of his contemporaries even regarded him as no more than a charlatan.

Yet he had his disciples, men and women who believed that they had learned much of value from the content of his writings, grossly exaggerated as we now know some of it was. There are, too, those in the late 20th century who think that Eliphas Lévi's influence has proved an abiding and valuable one. In a sense, the ghost of Apollonius, raised by Lévi well over a century ago, is still with us today, casting a long shadow.

He [Lévi] also came to believe that the ancient texts of alchemy... were written in a symbolic code; and that if he could only break this code, he would learn the ultimate secrets of the Universe...

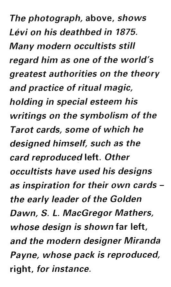

The photograph, above, shows Lévi on his deathbed in 1875. Many modern occultists still regard him as one of the world's greatest authorities on the theory and practice of ritual magic, holding in special esteem his writings on the symbolism of the Tarot cards, some of which he designed himself, such as the card reproduced left. Other occultists have used his designs as inspiration for their own cards – the early leader of the Golden Dawn, S. L. MacGregor Mathers, whose design is shown far left, and the modern designer Miranda Payne, whose pack is reproduced, right, for instance.

Young girls of the Caraya tribe of Peru, above, perform a dance for the Sun to mark the onset of puberty. If they did not take part in this age-old ritual, they would not be considered truly adult.

MAGICAL RITUALS HAVE BEEN PERFORMED SINCE TIME IMMEMORIAL AND ARE STILL USED TODAY – NOT JUST IN TRIBAL CULTURES BUT IN THE WEST, TOO – FOR GOOD AND FOR EVIL

The performing of rites – that is to say, cere-monial observances – probably plays a big-ger part in our lives than most of us realise. Even people who have never, for example, been present at a *barmitzvah*, the Jewish 'rite of pas-sage' that marks the transition from boyhood to manhood, or witnessed a celebration of the Christian Eucharist, have probably attended a twen-ty-first birthday party – the 'ceremonial observance' of the attainment of an adulthood that, in purely legal terms, is now reached some three years earli-er in some parts of the western world.

Indeed, from prehistoric graves, it is clear that our Stone Age ancestors carried out elaborate funeral rituals, and most primitive communities that

RITES AND WRONGS

out a similar rite with a toad, baptising it 'Jesus of Nazareth' and then crucifying it. Both rites seem to have been singularly ineffective.

If a clay doll, a wax image, or – as in the two strange Crowleyan rites mentioned above – an animal, is supposedly given the inner qualities of a particular living being by means of baptism or some other ceremonial observance, it is believed that a 'magical link' is established between the image and the living being. In some way, they have become mystically identified with one another, and anything that affects the image or animal will, so it is argued, affect its 'psychic twin' in a similar way.

In medieval times, if a peasant wanted to kill an enemy, he would make a realistic image of him and baptise it with the enemy's name. To make the psychic identification of image and enemy as close as possible, he would endeavour to obtain some hair and/or nail clippings of his intended victim and incorporate them into the statuette. He would then hammer nails or pins into the image or slowly destroy it, melting it over a slow fire, if it was made of wax, or putting it in a wet place, if it was made of clay. As the fire or water wasted away the image, so the body of the enemy would also, it was thought, waste away.

have survived into modern times seem to practise highly formalised and complex ceremonies to mark birth, puberty and death.

While it is impossible for us to know exactly what beliefs our early forbears held, it is likely that ritual was always associated with magic and the supernatural. A ceremony not only marked a particular event in life but in some way was often seen actually to produce that event. If, for example, a man or woman had not undergone the appropriate rituals associated with the attainment of adulthood, he or she was not considered a 'real adult', in spite of all appearances to the contrary.

Indeed, it was only a short mental step from thinking that sexually mature individuals were not adult humans because they had not been made adults by the appropriate rite to believing that certain ceremonies could also be used to turn some non-human entity (a tree or a clay image, for example) into a sort of honorary human being.

TASTE OF DECEPTION

Strange as such a mode of thinking may appear, it has persisted throughout history and has even survived into comparatively recent times. In the late medieval period, for instance, an abbot who yearned to eat meat during Lent was accused of adopting the ingenious device of baptising a sheep with the name of 'Carp', butchering it, and then eating it during the fast under the pleasant conviction that whatever appeared to be on his plate, it was in substance fish, not mutton.

During the 1930s, the fanatically anti-Christian occultist Aleister Crowley employed baptism in much the same way. He had a cockerel baptised with the name of John (the Baptist) and then solemnly beheaded it, in an elaborate ceremony based on Oscar Wilde's play Salome. This was supposed to destroy, in some mysterious way, the influence of Christianity upon the world. He carried

Dolls, or wax effigies have long been used as magical aids. A male and a female doll, above, bound together as if making love, are traditionally used to secure a lover. But darker thoughts inspired the doll, right, bound tightly, stabbed with pins and placed face down with a photograph and strands of hair of the intended victim. A sick mind may have devised it, but there is evidence that such 'games' can at times be deadly.

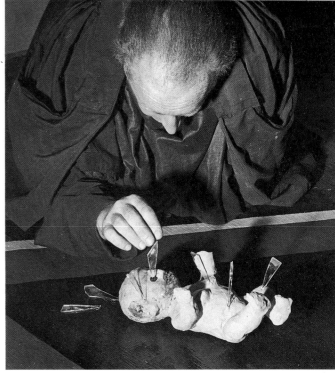

A similar, if more kindly intentioned process was often employed for sexual ends. A girl who desired a man would make images of herself and her beloved, incorporating, when possible, hair, nails, and bodily secretions and endowing the figures with prominent genitals in a state of sexual excitement. The images would be baptised with the appropriate names and then tied together with thread (usually red – a colour psychologically associated with sexual excitement), as though energetically copulating. Soon, it was hoped, the man's sexual desires would be directed towards the sorceress who, by this simple magical rite, would manage to capture his love.

MAGICAL LINKS

But were such magic rites actually effective? Sometimes, so it seems so, for there are well authenticated cases even in modern times, of the mysterious and medically inexplicable deaths of those who have been attacked by ritual magic involving the use of images. Exactly why these victims die is uncertain. It may be that there really is some 'magical link', created by ritual, between image and victim. Or it may be that the concentrated hate that the sorcerer pours out upon the image of his enemy telepathically exerts some form of destructive influence. More probably, it has been suggested, the victim is aware, or very strongly suspects, that ritual magic is being used by an enemy and kills himself by auto-suggestion – dying, quite literally, of fright.

Two stories from the 1930s that give support to this idea, but involving injury rather than death, were told by the American journalist William Seabrook. The first concerned a certain French concert pianist. (Seabrook called him Jean Dupuis to disguise his real identity.) A student of Rosicrucianism, astrology and other aspects of occultism, he had become involved with a dubious

A woman who sent a curse in the form of a letter to the Witches' Kitchen coven at Castletown, Isle of Man, provoked Cecil Williamson, the group's leader, to respond with all his painstaking art. First he made a 'poppet' to represent the woman who had cursed the coven; then he appealed to the spirits for power. Next, he breathed 'life' into the doll through a straw in its mouth, above left. Symbolically and, magicians believe, in some way actually, the doll had become the woman. Then Williamson inserted glass splinters into various parts of her body, above right. As long as the candles burned, she would 'feel torment sharper than the sting of needles'. In ritual magic, it is often the person with the greater hate – and ingenuity – who wins the psychic battle.

'esoteric group' with which he subsequently quarrelled. The group, angry at his defection, decided to destroy his ability to play by using a combination of ritual magic and applied psychology.

FIVE-FINGER EXERCISE

The magic came first. A doll was made in the image of Dupuis, baptised with his name and then clad in evening dress such as he wore on the concert platform. Its hands were then placed in a vice that was slowly tightened each day.

The psychology followed. Supposed friends of the victim – but in actuality, members of the group that was working against him – began to make comments and ask questions. His finger-work seemed less dextrous than usual, they remarked. Perhaps he was in need of a few days rest? Had he sprained his wrist, they enquired, or was he suffering from neuritis?

Within a week or two, these sly suggestions began to take effect. Jean Dupuis became excessively aware of his fingers, and his playing began to degenerate. Then, a few days before a concert, he received an anonymous note, beginning: 'I can tell you what is wrong with your hands, but it is so frightful that I am almost afraid to tell you'. The letter then proceeded to go into occult theories about magical links between images and men – matters that the writer knew the pianist had studied – and concluded by giving details of the doll with its hands held in a vice. On the night of the concert, a second note arrived: 'The handle of the vice will be slowly turned tonight, until your hands are crushed'.

The concert was a disaster: 'a false note, then a succession of jangling chords, followed by worse fumbling ... whispers and hisses from the outraged audience ... the young man half turned to the audience, resumed desperately; and, after a ghastly parody of the next few bars ... fled from the stage in shame and confusion.'

In this case, the victim was a student of the occult, a believer in ritual magic and its powers to hurt or kill. The other story told by Seabrook does, however, illustrate the fact that such sinister rites may sometimes exert an equally strong influence upon those who do not consciously believe in their efficacy, and would probably deny their power, if questioned.

In this instance, the victim was Louis, a French motor mechanic, the lover of a young girl whose peasant grandmother, a woman locally reputed to dabble in witchcraft, had taken an intense and unreasonable dislike to him. One day, Louis and the old woman quarrelled violently and almost came to blows. As the two parted – Louis to set off along a well-marked mountain path, the grandmother to return to her nearby cottage – the supposed witch began to chant an incantation:

'Tangled mind will twist and turn,
And tangled foot will follow . . .
So tangle, tangle, twist and turn,
For tangling webs are woven.'

By nightfall, Louis had not returned from his walk and a search party was sent out to hunt for him. He was found some distance from the path, entangled in briars, unable to walk, his legs paralysed. He said that he had wandered off the path, having become dizzy and increasingly confused, and he claimed that he had suffered some sort of stroke. He was ill, he continued to assert, even after the local doctor had been unable to find any physical injury to account for his condition.

Eventually Seabrook, convinced that ritual magic was responsible for Louis's condition, raided the old wine cellar in which the grandmother practised her witchcraft. On the floor he found laid out a miniature landscape, 'a tangled labyrinth of thorns and briars'. In its midst lay an image of Louis, with its eyes bandaged, and its feet tied and enmeshed in thorns and brambles.

Seabrook took the doll and showed it to Louis, who was annoyed that the old woman had attempted to harm him but still refused to accept that her activities had in any way been responsible for his paralysed state. 'I don't believe any of it,' he said, 'I've had a stroke.' His conscious mind, paradoxically enough, was lacking in the imaginative ability to

William B. Seabrook is seen above with the Ivory Coast forest people, including a young witch called Wamba. Seabrook travelled widely in the 1920s and discovered the universality of magical rites.

The extract, below, is a medieval magical incantation from the Key of Solomon – one of the most important of all grimoires.

understand the real cause of his paralysis. If he had been able to understand that primitive beliefs in sorcery and the supernatural lurked in the hidden depths of his own mind, he would probably once again have been able to walk.

These two cases represent only the most primitive strand in ritual magic, for the rites employed were extremely simple. As long ago as classical times, however, far more complex forms of ritual magic were evolved. The formulae, techniques and secrets of such elaborate occult systems are enshrined in the *grimoires* – textbooks of ceremonial magic.

" IT MAY BE THAT THERE REALLY IS SOME MAGICAL LINK, CREATED BY RITUAL, BETWEEN IMAGE AND VICTIM ... MORE PROBABLY, THE VICTIM IS AWARE OR VERY STRONGLY SUSPECTS THAT RITUAL MAGIC IS BEING USED BY AN ENEMY AND KILLS HIMSELF BY AUTO-SUGGESTION. "

Exactly when and where the first *grimoires* were compiled is uncertain. But something very like them existed in ancient Egypt; while magical works, many of them of Jewish origin, were circulated widely in the later centuries of the Roman Empire. It is probable that the European *grimoires* of the medieval period were derived from these, for they too show much evidence of Jewish influence. The authorship of many of them was attributed to King Solomon. According to legend, he was such a master of magic that he had dominion over men; demons, and even the angels of heaven.

The *Clavicula Salomonis* (Key of Solomon) and other magical works attributed to the great Jewish

SALOMONIS (CITATIO)

XYWOLEH.VAY.BAREC
HET.VAY.YOMAR.HA.ELOHE
ELOHIM.ASCHER.TYWOHE
HYTHALE.CHUABOTAY.LEP
HA.NAWABRA.HAMVEYS.HA
HAKLA.ELOHIM.HARO.HE
OTYMEO.DY.ADDHAYON
HAZZE.HAMALECH.HAGO

ELOTYMYCCOL.RAH.YEBA
RECH.ETHANEA.TYM.VEI
KA.REBA.HEM.SCHEMVE.EEL
SCHEMABO.TAY.ABRAHAM
VEY.SCHAK.VEYYD.GULA
ROBBE.KEREBHAARETZ.

CHAY.SEWAH.ANOCHY.YA
HEL.PARYM.BEWO.WYKAR
HIER NENNE DER GEISTER NAHMEN MIT IHREN (HEBRÆ) RUF, DIE DU HABEN WILLST, ZU DIENSTEN, AUS (DENEN) (NB) AMULETEN, UND NIMM IHR AMULET, LEGE ES VOR DICH HIN AUF DIE ERDE.

king display, like almost all the *grimoires,* a notable moral ambivalence. The hard core of the ritual magic of these works is the 'raising to visible appearance' of spirits, good and bad, with the object of obtaining benefits of one sort or another – usually wealth, power or knowledge.

The processes used fall into three stages: first, the preparation of the materials and implements to be used in the ceremony; secondly, the preparation of the magician's own mind and body; and thirdly, the actual performance of the rite.

The first of these stages involves the experimenter in compounding incense, moulding candles, and first manufacturing and then consecrating a variety of 'magical weapons', including a wand, a sword, and even a sickle. These processes are often extremely complex. One *grimoire,* for example, instructs the magician to forge his sickle one hour after sunrise on a Wednesday, bring it thrice to

A common, if melodramatic, image of the ritual magician summoning demons while standing in his magic circle is shown right. Essentially, the image is correct: a devoted magician will use ancient texts to summon up spirits and will often stand for hours inside a magic circle. He may indeed succeed in producing some entity – but it may be only an hallucination, visible only to him and owing its appearance more to the result of fasting and meditation than to the use of 'words of power'.

The photograph, **left,** *shows one of the images carved on the wall of a house at Bunbury, Cheshire, by a poacher who had been deported by the squire. On his return, the poacher carved three images to represent the squire and his two henchmen, and cursed them daily as witches do with dolls. The three men did indeed soon die.*

a red heat and then to immerse it in a mixture of herbal extracts and the blood of a magpie.

Another text tells the experimenter to build a stone altar on a river bank before dawn, behead a white cockerel at the moment of sunrise, throw its head in the river, drink its blood and burn its body. He must then jump into the river, climb out backwards, don new clothing and return to his dwelling.

Once the first two stages have been successfully accomplished, the magician can proceed to the ritual itself. He stands within a circle inscribed with names and symbols which are designed to protect him from demons who might wish to destroy him, and burns incenses, brandishing his magical implements, and chanting the lengthy and sonorous incantations given in the *grimoires.* Eventually, the spirit appears and gives the magician the things he desires, or so some occultists believe.

On the face of it, many of the processes involved in the ritual magic of the *grimoires* are so absurd – and often so repellent – that no normal person would wish to carry them out. This has led some modern occultists to deny that the texts of the *grimoires* are to be taken literally. These works, so it is argued, are written in a code only fully understandable by initiates. Thus, one *grimoire* teaches a method of giving someone a sleepless night: 'Pick a June lily under a waning moon, soak it in laurel juice and bury it in dung. Worms will breed therein. Dry them and scatter on your enemy's pillow'. This means, say those who believe the *grimoires* to be written in code, invoke the demons Lilith (the June lily) and Q'areb Zareg (the laurel), both of whom are reputed to give bad dreams.

Similar interpretations are employed by modern practitioners of ritual magic, who also take oaths to work in secret. There are, it is claimed, a surprising number of such exponents.

▮▮ IF A CLAY DOLL OR WAX IMAGE IS SUPPOSEDLY GIVEN THE INNER QUALITIES OF A HUMAN BEING BY MEANS OF SOME CEREMONIAL OBSERVANCE, IT IS BELIEVED THAT IN SOME WAY THEY HAVE BECOME MYSTICALLY LINKED WITH ONE ANOTHER, AND ANYTHING THAT AFFECTS THE IMAGE WILL AFFECT ITS 'PSYCHIC TWIN' IN A SIMILAR WAY. ▮▮